The Theory and Practice

of

GO

1. The Editors working over one of Korschelt's diagrams under the watchful eye of an expert. From left to right: Samuel P. King, Tameji Inagaki, George G. Leckie. In background, members of Hawaii's *Go*-playing community at a tournament held in January, 1964.

The Theory and Practice
of
GO

by
O. Korschelt

Translated and Edited by
SAMUEL P. KING & GEORGE G. LECKIE

CHARLES E. TUTTLE COMPANY: PUBLISHERS
Rutland, Vermont—Tokyo, Japan

Representatives:

Continental Europe: BOXERBOOKS, INC., *Zurich*
British Isles: PRENTICE-HALL INTERNATIONAL, INC., *London*
Australasia: BOOK WISE (AUSTRALIA) PTY. LTD.
104-108 Sussex Street, Sydney 2000

Published by the Charles E. Tuttle Company, Inc.
of Rutland, Vermont and Tokyo, Japan
with editorial offices at
Suido 1-chome 2-6, Bunkyo-ku, Tokyo

Copyright in Japan, 1965
by Charles E. Tuttle Co., Inc.

Library of Congress Catalog Card No. 65-22637
International Standard Book No. 0-8048-0572-5
First printing, 1966
Tenth printing, 1986

Book design by Simon Virgo
PRINTED IN JAPAN

Contents

Contents

EDITORS' PREFACE

As Korschelt suggests in his chapter on the evolution of *Go*, traditionally it was associated in Japan with politeness and politics, doubtless by virtue of the strategic insights afforded by its intuitive spontaneity and cumulative memory. Practical men cannot see objectively the events in which they are submerged without a neutral medium in which such events can be artificially manipulated and reflected. And, since the game is mentioned in Lady Murasaki's *The Tale of Genji* and the screen illustrations for this ancient book show games in progress, it has also been associated with poetry and calligraphy—that is, with works of love, for love is never far from the scene when the hero Genji is about.

In Japan's early cultural history, the antecedents of which extend back into ancient China, *Go* was one of the threads in the human fabric of ritual and magic. The combinations, in play, of white stones and black stones, along with the spatial structure of the game, constituted one of those dramatic forms or world-images marking the line of cleavage between man living in a state of myth and man in a state of science. At least, so the anthropologists now insist. With the fading of myth the heroic virtues retreat from man's way of seeing his world and existing in it. An archaic shadow lies just behind Korschelt's account of the history of *Go* and the changes it underwent towards the Meiji Restoration.

What is past is prologue, but it is not the intention of the Editors to deal with such exalted matters as poetry, politeness and politics here, let alone modern anthropology.

By the last quarter of the 19th century, during which period Korschelt wrote his analytic and systematic account of *Go*, it was well on the way in Japan to becoming a pure game of operational skill, guided by insights intrinsic to its own logic. Korschelt has dealt with this "pure" feature of the game so effectively, in his expository account, that his treatise was then and still remains a model for the game.

Indeed, if by *primary model* is meant one such that all future developments in its field reflect its formal structure and presuppositions, both explicit and implicit, then Korschelt's treatise stands to *Go* as Euclid's *Elements* stands to geometry. But in this connection one must remember that Korschelt had as his master, Murase Shuho (1838–1886 A.D.), the 18th Hon-In-Bo in a line of masters, about whom Korschelt speaks explicitly and to whose publications he certainly owes his last chapter on Openings, undoubtedly the most significant in his exposition.

That the above analogy (allowing for the actual differences) to Euclid is true the reader may prove for himself if he reads other books, subsequent to Korschelt's, on the game, whether in Japanese or some Western language. Today new geometries exist, of course; but the proper approach to understanding them still lies through Euclid, of which they are either developments or, in any case, complements. So also for Korschelt's treatise on *Go*.

Korschelt's treatise, along with the Japanese tradition that it embodies, is a classic in the strict sense of the term. Its interest is perennial and inexhaustible for the human imagination and understanding. It is this perennial potency that explains the essential reason for the Editors' efforts toward preparing an English edition from the German: that a distinguished Oriental game may become more widely distributed in the World; that the West may learn how to use its leisure wisely from this aspect of Japanese culture as it already has from other aspects.

The modern literary world seems largely convinced that a work of fiction must remain an enigma unless an exhaustive account of the author's familial affairs and hidden relations can be exposed to serve as a key. But the Editors do not believe that imposing the "Oedipus triangle" on Euclid would illuminate his *Elements*. Nor would such preoccupation advance the understanding of Korschelt. This is fortunate. For information about him seems quite meager. In connection with the articles which he wrote for learned publications, his name appears simply as *O. Korschelt*.

According to the GO MONTHLY REVIEW, *Vol. 3, No. 5, 1963,* a Japanese publication in English, "Korschelt was a German engineer who came to Japan at the invitation of the Japanese Government in the early part of the Meiji era (1867-1911). He worked at the Engineering Department of the Government as engineer on railroads." On the other hand, Dr. Kurt Meissner of Hamburg, author of *Deutsche in Japan 1639-1960,* has informed the Editors that Korschelt was an agronomist who was called to Japan through the agency of the Ministry for Agriculture and Commerce, to test and analyze soils; that he went to Japan in 1862 and stayed there until around 1882; and that his first name was Oscar. Furthermore it is known that he wrote an article entitled "The Water Supply of Tokyo," one "On Sake," one "On the Tenken System of Japanese Fortune Telling," and co-authored another on "The Chemistry of Japanese Lacquer."

Brief though these biographical details are, they do suggest a wide spectrum of interests. In Korschelt's time the primary task of the technologist was to apply, by way of invention, the theoretical models made possible by Galileo, Descartes and Newton to the description, manipulation and control of instrumental situations in nature as a field of motion and change. The technologist was the practical hero of the 19th century.

That Korschelt was a professionally educated German contributes toward explaining his zest for the systematic and analytic; that he was a technologist, his appreciation of the intuitive mobility of *Go,* of its spatial and combinatorial possibilities. This intersection of interests gave Korschelt's formulation of the game its exceptional character. For no matter how old a tradition is nor how rich its accumulation of experience, it does not formally come of age until it achieves a reflective understanding of itself as something freely produced in the world by an autonomous agent. This is its analytic period.

The present translation was made from the original German text. This text was supplied through a microfilm made by the Photoduplication Service of The Library of Congress, a directly readable copy having been later produced from the microfilm. The Service of the Library is herewith gratefully recognized.

The treatise appeared under the collective title: DAS "GO"-SPIEL. Its original medium of publication is fully described as follows: "MITTHEILUNGEN DER DEUTSCHEN GESELLSCHAFT FÜR NATUR-UND VÖLKERKUNDE OSTASIENS. Herausgegeben von dem Vorstande. BAND III (Heft 21-30 incl. nebst index) mit 10 Karten und 58 Tafeln. 1880-1884. Für Europa im Allein-Verlag von Asher & Co. Berlin W., unter den Linden 5. Yokohama Buchdruckerei des 'Écho du Japon.'" DAS "GO"-SPIEL appeared serially in the MITTHEILUNGEN, but limited to instalments 21-24.

The Deutschen Gesellschaft für Natur-und Völkerkunde Ostasiens was variously known as: The German Eastern-Asia Society and Doitsu Higashi-Azia Kenkyu

Kyokai (獨逸東亞細亞研究協會). The Society, established in 1873, had as its major purpose to study the countries and peoples of East Asia and to promote in the World a knowledge of these. Its secondary purpose was to promote scientific, cultural and social relations between Germany and the East Asiatic nations, especially Japan.

In arranging these articles as a book, the Editors have found it convenient to call the book *The Theory and Practice of Go*, that its name might conform more exactly with the nature of the treatise.

Publication in periodic form, along with a variety of other articles in each installment, must necessarily have limited the number of Plates, illustrating the formal operations of the game, which Korschelt could use, thus partially robbing his exposition of an important instrument. The Editors have remedied this defect by measurably extending the Plates beyond the ones given by Korschelt but actually indicated by his text. This feature should prove invaluable for elementary and intermediary students of the game.

Elizabeth S. Grilk of Exeter, New Hampshire, first rendered Korschelt into English out of family loyalty for one of the Editors and because of her affection for "scientific German." Her effort was of immense help and is duly acknowledged here.

Rebecca Berry brought order out of chaos as she typed and retyped the manuscript, for which the Editors are truly grateful.

Austin Shu, Chinese Cataloguer, Oriental Library, East-West Center, University of Hawaii, has provided invaluable help in regard to things Chinese.

Thanks are given to Tameji Inagaki, 6th Rank (amateur), and considered the strongest *Go* player in Hawaii, who gave authoritative solutions to some difficulties arising from misprints in the original articles and ambiguities in Korschelt's rhetoric.

As to the act of translation itself, somewhere Mark Twain has described a typical German sentence as like an endless freight train, of boxcar after boxcar of internal clauses, with the engine—the principal verb—pushing from the rear, puffing solemnly and patiently away. A powerful mechanism, this German engine, for those able to manipulate it. But modern English favors simplicity. The translator must, of course, seek every possible means that may serve to make the author speak intelligibly in his new medium, while simultaneously adhering faithfully to the author's intention.

As for any further comment on the act itself of translation, *qui s'excuse s'accuse* . . .

THE EDITORS: *Samuel P. King*
George G. Leckie

Honolulu, Hawaii
December, 1963

The Theory and Practice
of
GO

I

The Game of *Go*

Two PARTICULAR board games have been well known in Japan since ancient times. One is called *Shogi,* the other is called *Go*.

Shogi has certain features in common with chess, though it is less developed than chess as it is played in Europe.* *Shogi* has six kinds of officers in addition to the king and pawns, but the officers have very little freedom of movement. And in addition to the relative rigidity of the pieces there is a further obstruction to skill. In any unoccupied area one may choose, one may replace as one's own any pieces taken from an opponent. The basic lack of freedom of the pieces and the loose element of chance introduced by the rule of replacement make it impossible to plan any overall strategy effectively. These factors combine to make the level of skill in *Shogi* much inferior to what is possible in chess.[1]

---

*There is a brief description of the game by V. Holtz in the fifth number of MITTHEILUNGEN DER DEUTSCHEN GESELLSCHAFT FÜR NATUR-UND VÖLKERKUNDE OSTASIENS.

1 [References indicated by numerals throughout the text are located at the end of the book. *Eds.*]

Despite its inherent limitations, however, *Shogi* does belong to a much higher level of skill than the common board games, such as checkers and mill,[2] as we usually play them. Skill at *Shogi* is a commonplace all over Japan. One sees lively games of *Shogi* going on everywhere at almost any time. The fact that card playing is stringently outlawed[3] probably contributes to its popularity. Still, no systematic exposition of the game has ever been formulated, nor, as V. Holtz says, have there been any *Shogi* clubs. And I do not know of any book of any sort about *Shogi*.

But when one reflects upon the other Japanese board game called *Go,* the historical and strategic picture typical of *Shogi* is replaced by another that is decidedly different in several respects. Eleven centuries have elapsed[4] since the game was first brought over from China. During this time the Japanese have elaborated and developed its strategy with tireless energy. Because of such dedication the Japanese developed a style of play that was so fluent and resourceful that they eventually outstripped the Chinese at the game. Today *Go* is regarded as something as much Japanese as anything else of that character.[5]

Japan's major interest in *Go* is effectively illustrated by the fact that for the last three centuries the development of *Go* and its explicit formulation as an advanced study has been a part of governmental policy. A *Go* Academy was established and maintained throughout the period.

Expert players, who received good salaries as administrative officials, were employed and entrusted with the responsibility of teaching and developing the game as an organized art.

Although the Academy finally fell apart in 1868, along with the other administrative institutions of the broken Shogunate, it had by that time accomplished its work well. It had brought forward a copious body of recorded observations about the art of *Go* and had so much improved the game that no apologies need be made for it in comparison with European chess. True, despite its great worth, none among the locally resident foreigners has ever thoroughly mastered the game. But the causes behind this are rather more accidental than essential. The initial or elementary steps are tedious, and to advance requires a decided continuity of effort and a not inconsiderable practice in order to become a good player in even a preliminary sense.

Our European manuals present the game of chess in systematic and abstract terms, but one does not find this style in the Japanese books about *Go*. Collections of exemplary games presented through diagrams do exist, but the commentary is in the form of marginal notes that are both few and much condensed, usually pointing out that this or that move was well or ill made in relation to the overall strategy. No matter what important insights these notes may carry, they are so abbreviated that a beginner can get no help from them. The result is that in the absence of an adequate manual that might serve to guide one directly into the heart of the game, one must make a patient and long approach by means of step-by-step practice and of face-to-face instruction with a master of the game.

A long illness allowed me time enough to get through the tedious elementary stages of the game. Then, later, benefiting further from the instruction of Japan's top master of Go,[6] I got on far enough to see what an excellent game Go really is and that its level of skill is a challenge to chess. I am convinced that only one thing is needed in order to make the game appreciated in Europe, and that is a well and fully explicated formulary of its strategy. Our chess circles would recognize that the ingenuity and depth of skill in Go are fully a match for chess, and it would soon be cherished as highly as chess.

Chess and Go are both antagonistic or warlike games, that is, they are both governed primarily by skill in tactics and strategy. But the form of conflict typical of chess is like the warfare of olden times in which the king was the center of the struggle and the battle was lost with his downfall. In this sort of knightly struggle victory or defeat was decided more through the exceptional virtue of a single noble or group of nobles than through the mass action of the commoners as parts of an overall strategy.

Rather than being the image of a single struggle as in chess, Go is much more like the panorama of an entire campaign or complex theater of war. And so it is more like modern warfare where strategic mass movements are the ultimate determinants of victory. Engagements are regularly carried out on various parts of the board either simultaneously or in sequence, strongholds or fixed positions are beleaguered and overcome, entire armies are forced from their line of defense and captured unless they fortify themselves quickly enough in unassailable positions. As in modern warfare, direct combat, without supporting tactics, rarely occurs. In fact, to engage too soon in direct combat frequently spells defeat. Comprehensive strategy and only comprehensive strategy makes victory certain.

Whether chess or *Go* offers more entertainment is a difficult question. Unlike chess the combinations in *Go* are afflicted with some monotony because there are no pieces with different styles of movement and because once placed in the field the stones are fixed. But that defect is compensated for by the greater ratio of combinations and by the greater number of places on the board where the battle may rage. In general, two average players of fairly even skill will find more enjoyment in *Go* than in chess. In chess it is fairly certain that the first of two evenly matched players to lose a piece will suffer defeat unless he can exchange it for one of like value. Without such an exchange after a loss the rest of the game is mostly an ineffective struggle against predictable defeat. The player with the advantage has only to protect himself against making an error to keep his advantage. But in *Go* an occasion of greater loss need not spell defeat in the long run. One simply shifts to another area of battle where the prior misfortune is usually irrelevant and there his wound may be revenged.

Indeed, a nice feature of *Go* in contrast with chess is that a severe loss in the early game can become a means towards securing a considerable advantage in another sector of the board. This is accomplished by the exploitation of the so-called *Ko* situation which will be explained later. Any game is the more interesting the more often the prospects of victory or defeat shift and the less certain it is that any momentary superiority, inflexibly limiting the final chances of victory, can be maintained until the end. This trembling of chance in the balance of skill provides the excitement that sustains card playing. The odds do not shift often in chess, rarely more than twice, but in *Go* the possibilities are much greater.

Even in the end game of *Go,* and often enough in the last dramatic moments of play, the threatening cloud of certain defeat may be dispersed by a resourceful maneuver that leads to a brilliant victory. Although, just as much as in chess, *Go* is a game in which the chance fall of luck plays no essential part, but only circumspection and finesse, still it can be played with more excitement than chess and its style is just in that measure more interesting.

II
The History of *Go**

Go IS THE oldest of known games. Its invention is assigned in ancient Chinese sources to three different persons. But the Japanese commonly only regard one of them as the true inventor, namely, the famous Chinese Emperor Shun, who reigned from 2255 to 2205 B.C.[7] Reckoned from this date, the game is forty-one centuries old. It is said he founded the game that his son San Chun might alleviate his weak-mindedness through playing it. Others designate Shun's predecessor, the Emperor Yao, who reigned from 2356 to 2255 B.C., as the founder, an increase of a century in the age of the game. A third notion is that Wu, a vassal of the Emperor Chieh, who reigned from 1818 to 1766 B.C., originated *Go,* and thus the game would be thirty-seven centuries old.

Miyoshi rather thinks that Yao or Shun may have been the inventor and that Wu rediscovered it later—an incident not unusual in the history of inventions. I favor the

*Mr. Miyoshi, an official in the Ministry of Finance, learned in both Chinese and *Go,* has at my request been so good as to write for me a "History of *Go*" from which the conjectures of this section have been taken.

third position: first, because the discovery would be more recent; second, because Wu was an underling, not an emperor. It is not given to emperors to have either the time or the opportunity to discover anything new—then as now.

Aside from such details, Miyoshi is of the opinion that, though it is only sensible to be doubtful about ancient reports, it is quite probable that *Go* was known among the Chinese in early times. He cites a number of ancient Chinese sources to support his contention. The oldest is from about 1000 B.C.—some thirteen centuries after Yao and Shun—in which a game like *Go* is referred to parenthetically. All in all, the above suppositions about the antiquity of *Go* seem reasonable.

As is known, chess was also once believed to be of immense age. It was confused with an Indian game, involving the use of dice, in which four persons played. Each player had eight pieces (such as king, elephant, horse and foot-soldier) and it was played on a board. A cast of dice was used to determine which pieces were to be moved. The supposition is that chess later developed from this game. Chess as we know it first arose around 500 A.D. At that time, the pieces, in part, still had quite unfree movements, and it was not until about the 15th century that chess approached the present stage of its form.

In this general context it is entirely reasonable to suppose that *Go* underwent a similar development toward increasing completeness. If this were true, one could not attribute to *Go* any such antiquity as four thousand years. An inference of that sort by analogy, however, about its development is not valid because of the fact that the rules for *Go* are without parallel in their simplicity. A look at the rules, given in the next chapter, will convince the reader that the games must be few that have simpler rules. Improvements have been made in one aspect only. The game arrived only gradually at the present physical spread of the board—probably the best in terms of the purpose—with its 19 × 19 arrangement of lines and the thereby proportionately conditioned present sum of playing stones. But partial changes of that sort no more radically altered the character of the game than a new game was created when certain chess pieces were given modified movements some four hundred years ago. The conclusion is that *Go* is indeed four thousand years old and so the world's oldest game.

Miyoshi also says that in China from about 200 B.C.– 600 A.D. poetry and *Go* both enjoyed a golden age together. The poet Ma Yung, who flourished about 240 A.D.,* made himself famous in the land by the poems in which he magnified the name of *Go*.

It is mentioned in the old books, and as something remarkable, that in the 3rd century A.D. a certain Osan was so skilled at *Go* that he could sweep a finished game from the board and then set it up again correctly entirely from memory. This is of especial interest because it shows

*[c. 79–166 A.D. *Eds.*]

that in the course of time the schooling of memory has resulted in making such powers of recollection a necessary condition for expert skill at *Go*. Today hundreds of players in Japan can tear down a completed game and then set it back up step by step. In fact, when a learner is playing with a teacher it is customary for the master to reconstruct the game play by play in order to comment on the learner's progress.

Many anecdotes about *Go* have survived from ancient Chinese times. One of these shows well how highly the game was then regarded. A certain Hsieh An, who lived during the Tsin Dynasty (265-420 A.D.) was at war with his nephew Hsieh Hsüan. After a considerable amount of bloodshed, they decided to let the outcome of their antagonism rest on the disposition of a game of *Go*, which they played against one another.

The most accomplished players were honored with such titles as *Ki-sei* or *Ki-sen* (from *Ki*=the game of *Go*, and *Sei*=Holy One, or *Sen*=a magic creature dwelling in the mountains).

The first books, such as *Gokyo* and *Gosetsu*, about *Go* were written during the T'ang Dynasty (618-906 A.D.) and Sung Dynasty (960-1126 A.D.). *Go* blossomed during this period in China, and there were many distinguished players.

In the 6th year of Tempyo Shoho (according to the Japanese system), under the rule of Empress Koken, or in the 13th year of the Emperor Yüan Tsung (according to the Chinese system), *Go* was brought to Japan, and a new epoch opened for the game. According to our system of chronology this was 754 A.D. At that time the celebrated personage Kibidaijin was sent to China as ambassador. He brought the game back to Japan. But the game spread slowly. After a century, by report, the number of players among the nobles—for the game was restricted to the nobility—was small.

In the periods Kasho (848-851 A.D.) and Ninju (851-854 A.D.) a Japanese prince who was living in China is said to have played the game a great deal. He had as his teacher a certain Koshigen, reputed to have been the best of Chinese players. A well-known story, which I have often heard, relates that as a matter of protocol the best players were always assigned as his opponents. In order to meet this difficult situation he hit upon the expedient of placing his pieces just as his opponents did, with the result that he finally won the game. That is, when his opponent placed a stone at any point, the prince placed his in an exactly corresponding spot and so triumphed. But if the Chinese were as easily gulled as that and unable to find the obvious remedies, they must have been mediocre players, after all. It is only necessary to place a stone on the board's center, which has no corresponding point, or so manipulate the game as to take an opponent's central stone in order to spoil such a symmetrical style of game.

It was around 850 A.D. that Wakino Ason Sadaomi

became famed as a great friend of *Go*. Playing night and day through, he became so totally lost in the game as to be unaware of anything else.

For the next two centuries skill at *Go* did not extend beyond the bounds of the Imperial Court at Kyoto; indeed, it seems that the game was officially confined to the Court. At least, Miyoshi claims that in the period Otoku (1084-1086 A.D.) the Prince of Dewa, Kiyowara Iehira, smuggled the game into Oshu [Mutsu] and Dewa and played it there with his retainers. From that time on not only did players among the nobles increase briskly; but also the well-to-do from among the people began the study of *Go*. By the first part of the 13th century *Go* was commonly known among the military. It was played with enthusiasm. All ranks, from the time's most famous generals to the lowest soldiers, who went to war, played *Go*. Board and stones went to the battlefield. No sooner was an engagement over than out they came and the game of war-in-peace was on.

In Kamakura, which Minamoto no Yoritomo had raised to the rank of a court seat in 1186 A.D., Hojo Yoshitoki had once just begun a game with a guest when he received news of Wada Yoshimori's defection.[8] Yoshitoki first finished the game in utmost serenity. It was only then that he turned his attention to the necessary measures for putting down the revolt. This happened in the 1st year of Kempo (1213 A.D.). A similar story is told about Taira no Nobunaga, also called

Oda Nobunaga, which shows that he, like all of the great Japanese heroes, was also devoted to *Go*. He came to Kyoto in the 10th year of Tensho (1582 A.D.), and lodged in the Honno-ji Temple. Calling the famous *Go* player Sansha into his presence, he played with him until midnight. Upon leaving, Sansha was hardly out of the house before Akechi Mitsuhide's uprising broke out.

Even before Nobunaga's time both poets and monks esteemed *Go* and many names from among them are listed as famous *Go* players.

In the periods Genki (1570-1572 A.D.), Tensho (1573-1592 A.D.) on to Keicho (1596-1614 A.D.) and Genwa (1615-1623 A.D.) there were numerous monks, poets, burghers and merchants who became widely celebrated because of their skill at *Go*. Such players were summoned to the courts of the *daimyo,* and of the other nobility, to play with their hosts or often just to exhibit their skill. This practice of arranging exhibitions still holds today.[9] *Go* enthusiasts join together to invite two famous experts to put on a professional game. The onlookers are so attentive and still during the pauses, which are often painfully long, show such admiration of the masterful strokes, make such an intense effort to grasp the problems in depth, and are so absorbed throughout the play that I am, again and again, astonished every time I witness one of these exhibition matches. Except within the confines of chess circles nothing of this sort is found in our social world. But in Japan much wider social communities develop an interest in *Go*. An appreciation of the game is properly a sign of social finesse.

That watching expert *Go*-playing is a pleasurable pastime for so many of the Japanese is proof positive that they are a highly cultivated people. Only a highly cultivated people could find pleasure in such an intense procedure that, at the same time, is free from any sensual distraction.

At the beginning of the 17th century *Go* both developed and spread rapidly. A great number of expert players gradually appeared who far surpassed in skill all of their predecessors. The most distinguished of these were Hon-In-Bo Sansha Hoin,[10] Nakamura Doseki, Hayashi Rigen, Inouye Inseki and Yasui Santetsu. Sansha was originally a monk who had been admitted as a dweller in the Shukuko-ji Temple which was one of the sixteen principal temples in Kyoto for the Nichiren Sect of Buddhism. Skilled in *Go* since his youth, he eventually gave up his religious status, and obtained permission to start a center for teaching *Go* (*Go-dokoro*). At this change of vocation he renamed himself Hon-In-Bo Sansha. He was soon frequently seen in the company of Nobunaga, Toyotomi Hideyoshi, and Tokugawa Ieyasu, Japan's three most eminent men. All three of them delighted in playing *Go* during such free hours as their political activities allowed. Hon-In-Bo often went with them on their travels and campaigns and so was a witness to not a few of the period's historical battles. The center for teaching *Go*, however, was Hon-In-Bo's own enterprise, not government supported.

A state-supported school for *Go* is said to have been first established by Toyotomi Hideyoshi in the period Tensho (1573-1592 A.D.). But it seems to have had a short life, for Miyoshi speaks—unfortunately without giving the year of its founding—of another government school for *Go* established by the Shogun Tokugawa Ieyasu. Since Ieyasu became Shogun in 1603 A.D. the founding of the *Go-in* or *Go* Academy must have followed shortly afterward. Hon-In-Bo Sansha as Japan's outstanding *Go* player was appointed head of the Academy and received 350 *tsubo*[11] of land and 200 *koku* of rice yearly. Other master players were installed as instructors and assigned good salaries.

With the founding of the Academy the most gifted players of the period, freed from the distraction of earning a living, could now devote themselves entirely to the advancement of pupils as well as to the further development of the game. The Academy was equally successful in achieving both purposes. Its graduates were everywhere much more accomplished *Go* players than the older generation had been. They practiced the game professionally as a means of livelihood, finding either a post at the court of some *daimyo* or else wandering over the land—like the itinerant poets and sword masters of the period—stopping here and there, wherever they found a favorable reception, to play and to give instruction in *Go*, matching their skill with that of the finest local players. If they came to a place that was finally pleasing, they put their questing years behind them and settled there, earning their living by teaching the game.

When the *Go* Academy was founded, in addition to Hon-In-Bo, the masters Hayashi, Inouye and Yasui mentioned above were called as teachers. There is no further record of Nakamura for some unknown reason. Each of these four masters founded his own style and tradition of playing independently of the others, and thus in this sense one speaks of schools of *Go*. It was customary for each master to adopt his outstanding pupil who at his death inherited his position. This is why the masters of the Academy were always named Hon-In-Bo, Inouye, Hayashi or Yasui.[12]

The best players of the *Go* Academy were required to appear and play before the Shogun every year. To insure that this ceremony, called *Go-zen-go* (the Game before the August Presence), should not run on too long, the moves were carefully studied out and rehearsed in advance. This custom continued until the abolition of the Shogunate (1868 A.D.), when both *Go-zen-go* and the *Go* Academy came to an end together.

At the founding of the Academy, Hon-In-Bo Sansha established an ascending scale of degrees for its graduates which is in use today. Whoever reached a certain determinate level of proficiency received the title *Sho-dan*[13] or (player of the) First Rank, still better players being, in order, *Ni-dan, San-dan, Yo-dan,* that is, Second Rank, Third Rank, Fourth Rank, etc. The highest rank ever reached is *Ku-dan,* or Ninth Rank. A *Sho-dan* is skillful enough to follow the game as a profession. In any other game such an accurate scale would hardly be possible, but in *Go* the better player regularly wins, even though his advantage in skill may be only slight.

If it were not possible to balance the different degrees of skill among players in some way, most games would be tedious because the weaker of the two players would have nothing to look forward to but certain defeat. The stronger player always gives his opponent in advance whatever number of stones are needed as a handicap to put the two players in approximate balance with each other. Thus my teacher, Mr. Murase Shuho,[14] the best contemporary player in Japan and a *Shichi-dan* or Seventh Rank, now gives me seven stones but usually defeats me anyway. At the beginning of my instruction, after I had just learned the rudiments of the game, he gave me thirteen stones and always beat me in spite of the handi-cap. It is not usual to give more than thirteen stones; if a player needed more, the gap between the two players would be so great that the game would be tiresome. By way of comparison, a First Rank player receives an ad-vantage of three stones from a Seventh Rank player.

Handicap stones are placed on certain specified spots on the *Go* board, which are distinguished by small black dots. At least, this is so when one receives an advantage of two or more stones, for an advantage of one stone received by the player with the Black stones, who must move first, is not considered a handicap stone and may be played on any chosen point. Otherwise, the placing of the handicap stones is considered as a play.

A player of the Seventh Rank in addition has the title *Jo-zu* or top-hand, one of the Eighth Rank, *Kan-shu* or middle-hand, and one of the Ninth Rank, *Mei-shu* or clear-bright-hand as well as *Mei-jin* or famous person. In the nearly three centuries since this way of ranking *Go* players was established, there have been no more than nine persons of the Ninth Rank, likewise nine of the Eighth Rank, but many of the Seventh Rank and many times more in all the lower ranks. Today there is in all Japan only one player who has climbed as high as the Seventh Rank, in contrast to some two hundred of the First Rank.

An ascending scale of this sort for ranking *Go* players is quite unknown in either China or Korea, although it is used in the Ryukyu Islands.

Japanese *Go* players, apparently, look upon this scale of merit as rigidly fixed. But in a quantitative situation of this sort where the standard of comparison or unit of measurement cannot be exact, the scale can only be relative and from time to time subject to displacement. And obviously the standard must have become, during the course of the centuries, slowly steeper.

Players of higher rank who bestow the lower grades upon aggressive aspirants—as is done in Germany in regard to doctoral candidates—or who have to recognize urgently ambitious players of a hitherto lower rank as equals in play, be they ever so impartial in intention, will unconsciously tend to hinder somewhat the advancement of newcomers. For if the players of higher rank are surpassed or if too much fresh competition threatens, their fame which is their most precious possession is placed in jeopardy. A high ranking player will not concede equality to a rising contender until the other has already become somewhat stronger than he is himself.

And even if it happens that testing for degrees is ever so impartial, each player would actually gain greater skill through practice although each should keep the same rank relative to the others. Today's Seventh Rank player would become stronger after a year of practice, even if at the end of that interval he were still classed formally as a player of the Seventh Rank. Because of this tendency for the standard of perfection to shift upwards it must have eventually come about that today a player of the Seventh Rank can play quite as well as, or perhaps better than, a player of the Eighth Rank or Ninth Rank a century or two ago. I can cite a convincing example to show that this is what has happened.

The Ryukyu Islands have had the same order of grading for a long time, probably since soon after its establishment in Japan, and then, as far as *Go* is concerned, they

lost touch with Japan and were again first visited by a *Go*
player, from Satsuma, two years ago. For an interval of
two centuries the order of merit for *Go* stood almost still
in the Ryukyu Islands. Since throughout this period of
isolation from *Go* players of Japan only very few good
players would have developed on the island there would
have been less opportunity there than in Japan to confer
degrees and in this way to upgrade the standard of perfection. Thus the standard in the Ryukyu Islands would
have advanced some, but not nearly so much as on the
Japanese mainland. This was actually the case. The
Second Rank *Go* player from Satsuma found a *Go* player
in the islands who claimed to be of the Fifth Rank and
the best player in the area. But the Satsuman defeated
him and thus showed that he was, at most, a weak player
of the Second Rank. The Satsuman along with the other
high ranking *Go* players in Japan charged the Ryukyu
people with being empty boasters for arrogating to themselves higher levels of perfection than they had properly
earned.

In the first half of this [the 19th] century the game
of *Go* took a fresh surge forward, which according
to Japanese reckoning fell in the periods Bunka (1804-
1818 A.D.), Bunsei (1818-1830 A.D.) and Tempo (1830-
1844 A.D.). The exemplary games collected from this
period are still regarded today as models. The period's
style of play and openings are still used and have not
been fully replaced by others. The best collections of

exemplary games were originated by Hon-In-Bo Dosaku, Hon-In-Bo Jowa and Yasui Sanchi. From that time up to the present, the collections inherited from Hon-In-Bo Shuwa have been of the greatest interest and are valued as among the best that was achieved.

In 1868 A.D. the *Go* Academy closed and state sponsorship for the game ended. Even the *daimyo*, who were dispossessed some few years afterward, felt, in their private capacity, no further motivation to support court players of *Go*. So, hard times fell upon the *Go* masters, who had lived for the most part by their skill at *Go*, and to make matters worse even the people lost interest in the game. After the opening of Japan to foreign entry, everyone turned with enthusiasm to things alien, prized more highly than native things because they were newly fashionable, and so neglected Japan's ancestral heritage.

But in the last few years a healthy reaction has set in against the intemperate desertion of things legitimately Japanese and as a part of this reaction interest has revived in the characteristically Japanese game, and now *Go* is again as much alive as it ever was. The younger generation has applied itself to the study of foreign languages and science and hardly plays it at all, but *Go* is carried on with just that much more interest by the civil service. Most high ranking state officials are ardent players and Vice-Premier Iwakura is held to be one of the best. Though the game is played in the Army, it is especially beloved in the Navy. The four schools of style in *Go* playing, those of Hon-In-Bo, Inouye, Hayashi and Yasui, were still in existence after 1868 A.D., but without government support.

At this intersection of events, in March of 1879 A.D., Murase Shuho carried out a *coup d'état* that severely shook up the two hundred and fifty year old constitution of the game. He belonged to the Inouye school, but he was a stronger player than the then incumbent head who was only of the Sixth Rank while Murase himself was of the Seventh Rank. The old usages had lost their meaning for him so there was no further point in his waiting for an empty promotion, and less so since he had already achieved the highest fame that he could reach in his lifetime, namely that of being the best *Go* player in the country. He left the Inouye school and collected a number of good players about himself as a new center.

This group met monthly to play, each member playing one game, which sometimes lasted for as much as twenty-four hours without a break. Murase later published these games with the addition of a few brief critical comments. The most notable among these younger players was Nakamura, of the Sixth Rank, whose style of play was exceptionally resourceful and whose games, like Murase's, often contained problems of great refinement. Nakamura was distinguished especially for his daring style of attack, while Murase remained equally composed and relaxed whether in attack or defense.

Whereas in Japan, in good part through state support, *Go* has reached a high stage of development, in China, its motherland, it seems to be in a state of decay. The Japanese players certify that there is not a single player in China who is the equal of a Japanese player of the First Rank.

In Möllendorff's *Chinese Bibliography*[15] there is no reference to *Go,* though references to Chinese chess are rather plentiful. If the Chinese placed any sort of value upon the game, certainly something would have been written about it.

III

The Rules of Play

THE BOARD consists of a rectangular block of wood, usually *Salisburia*,[16] as free of knots as possible, about 44 cm. long, 40½ cm. wide and 12 cm. high. Four feet are set into the bottom of the board so that overall it stands about 20 cm. high. The players customarily are seated on floor mats with the board between them. Some boards are constructed about 3½ cm. thick and without feet, suitable for use on tables now that they have been introduced into Japan. On the board parallel to the two sets of sides are drawn two sets of 19 black lines, each line being about 1 mm. thick. In one direction the lines are somewhat farther apart than in the other so that the areas constructed by the intersecting lines are still right-angled parallelograms but not strictly squares, though they do approach closely to being squares. Regarded as a whole, the field is a rectangle whose sides are 38½ × 42 cm. In play the board is customarily so placed that the narrow sides face the players. The stones are placed on the points where the lines intersect, as in mill, and *not* in the spaces, as in chess and checkers. The total number of stones is the same as the total number of intersects, that is, 19 × 19

$= 361$, and these are divided into 180 White stones and 181 Black stones.

The White stones are made of mussel shell and the Black stones are made of slate or of basalt darkened with lamp-black. The form of the stones is approximately that of a convex lens but, it seems, intentionally somewhat irregular. There are also stones baked from fire-clay, but one never typically finds these in use, though the others are more costly. The White stones are usually somewhat larger than the Black and both are larger than the board requires. Thus my Black stones are about 17/16 of the distance between the vertical lines of the board and about 18/19 of the distance between the horizontal lines, and my White stones are about 13/12 of the distance between the vertical lines and about 36/37 of the distance between the horizontal lines. The result is that in play there is not enough room for the stones to lie side by side in an orderly way and so they push each other about and even out of line. The resulting irregular appearance is deliberately increased further in that players hardly trouble to place the stones exactly on their proper points, but, on the contrary place them so loosely that sometimes one can hardly grasp the overall aspect of the game. Artifice of this sort is presumably introduced to break the apparent monotony of the game which would suffer from too much superficial symmetry if the scene-in-play area were perfectly rectilinear and if the stones were to fit in exactly, were fully regular and stood precisely on their points of play.

I wish to remark that if *Go* boards are to be made in Europe, cardboard should not be used. When the stone is taken between the tips of the thumb and forefinger, or held loosely between the fore and middle finger as the Japanese prefer, and then brought down with a smart rap on a hard wooden board, a cheerful ringing note follows. But on cardboard the effect is quite dull and flat. A small, marble-topped table, with the lines incised on its surface, had best be used for a board. Suitable White stones could be made out of mussel shells which would be light and agreeable in texture to the sense of touch; and indeed glazed porcelain would perhaps do very well for both the Black and the White stones.

As mentioned previously, the rules are very simple. They derive entirely from the operative principle that each of the two players in turn places one of his stones on a free point not yet occupied. Except in one situation, to be described later, a player is fully free in his choice of which point to occupy. The formal intention of the game is to bind gradually into chains the separate stones which from the opening game have been placed upon different sections of the field so as to enclose as many free or vacant parts of the field as possible. One continues in turn to play stones until all the gaps in the White or Black chains as well as all the vacant areas between the White and Black chains are filled up. Then the play comes to an end and the free points that remain unoccupied inside the chains are counted. The one who has the most such free points is the victor. In counting these unoccupied points the rule is that each player shall count, not his own points, but those of his opponent. In order to avoid any possible error, the stones are so rearranged that the free points appear as ordered in rows of five or ten. Plates 2 and 4 each show a finished game. Each is respectively rearranged in Plates 3 and 5. In Plate 3, White has 54 free points, Black 55, so Black wins by one point. In Plate 5, White has 58 free points, Black 56, and hence, White wins by 2 points.

If a stone is surrounded on four sides by an opponent's stones as shown by Plate 6 diagram (a), it is termed "killed" or "dead," and is taken from the field by the opponent. In Plate 6 diagrams (b) and (c) the Black stones are thus killed. In all three examples only the stones essentially necessary for the death predicament are shown, though actually one customarily uses supporting stones to protect the surrounding ones. Thus Plate 6 diagram (c) in actual play would look like Plate 6 diagram (f) where two further supporting stones have been added. To surround a stone in the open field, four stones are needed as in Plate 6 diagram (a); if it is on the edge, the opponent needs three stones, as in Plate 6 diagram (d); if in a corner, only two, as in Plate 6 diagram (g).

The only exception, limiting what is otherwise a complete freedom of point choice, is a restriction in connection with the so-called *Ko* situation. Plate 6 diagrams (e) and (h) show the sequence of plays which gives rise to its

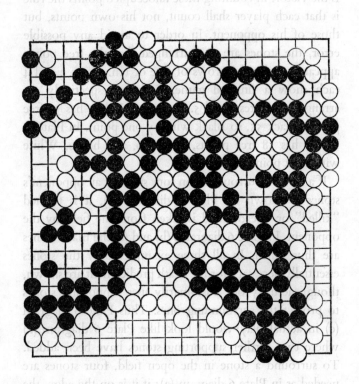

Plate 2

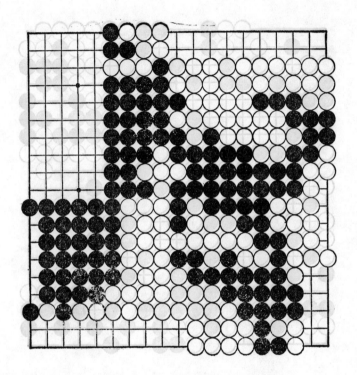

Plate 3

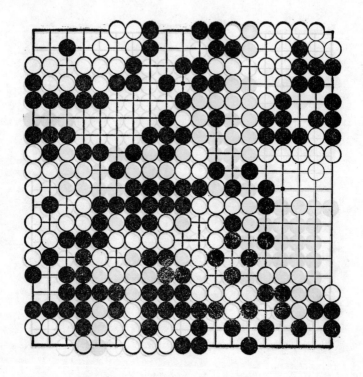

Plate 4

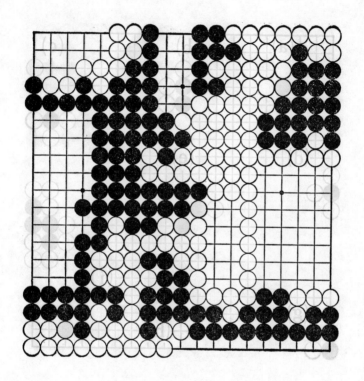

Plate 5

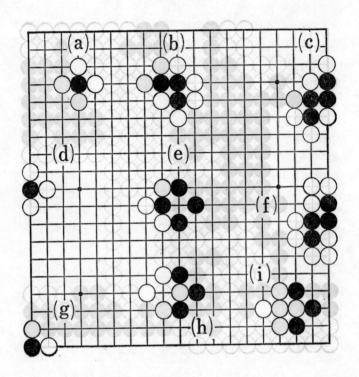

Plate 6

application. If it is, say, White's turn to play, he can take the Black stone, for it is already enclosed on three sides. This gives rise to the situation shown in Plate 6 diagram (h). But now the newly placed White stone is likewise threatened on three sides and, since Black's move is next, can be taken in turn. But Black is proscribed from making this play and instead must make a play elsewhere on the board. White now has a true choice: either to counter Black's new move elsewhere on the board or to stabilize the *Ko* situation. If he chooses the latter tactic, the formation shown in Plate 6 diagram (i) results.

The reason for the one restrictive rule is not far to seek. If an immediate re-take were permitted, and the winning or losing of the game turned around the possession of this point, the game could never be concluded because the players could take and re-take endlessly. The ideogram represented here by the romanized Japanese word *Ko* means talent, skill or a deserving meritorious deed.[17] Since, in fact, as will be shown later, a player's true aptitude for the game can be shown by the way he handles *Ko*, the name is well chosen for the situation described. If a player, however, takes more than one stone at a play, resulting in his capturing stone being left surrounded on three sides, the opponent can then take it immediately because this situation does not give rise to an endless exchange. Plate 7 diagrams (a), (b) and (c) show an example of this situation.

Not infrequently, when stones have been consolidated

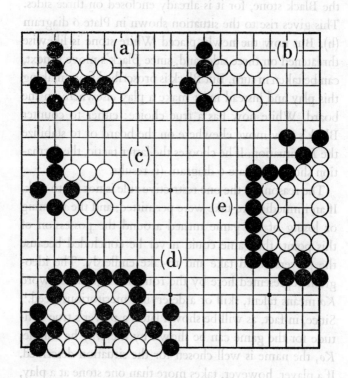

Plate 7

into chains, some of an opponent's stones which he did not find the opportunity to complete into a chain after starting one are found caught inside of the hostile enclosure. Such stones are considered killed even without being strictly enclosed on all sides, and are taken at the end of the game from their locations and placed on free points inside the areas enclosed by the opponent's chains. The same disposition is made of stones killed during the game and removed from the board. Each killed stone is equivalent to two points, moreover, for the point which the stone had occupied remains free for the player making the capture and at the end of the game the stone occupies a specific point in the opponent's territory that otherwise would be free.

In Plate 4 are shown two examples of stones that were surrounded by an opponent's chains before their player had time to rescue them. As one can see in the upper left corner there is in the small White chain a Black stone that is not tightly surrounded by the White stones.* And in the large White chain on the right side too are twelve Black stones which are dead, in effect, because their connection with the other nearest Black stones has been cut off.

Often one can manage to tie such threatened stones into a chain which encloses some free points but not enough to withstand an enveloping attack from both outside and within by a knowledgeable opponent. The White chain

*[The White position is not yet safe. *Eds.*]

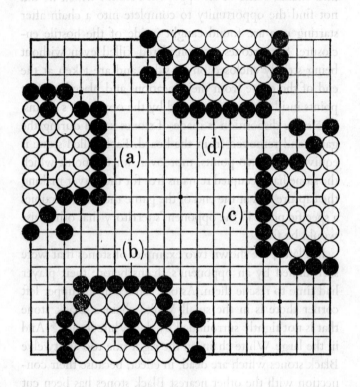

Plate 8

on the left edge of Plate 4 exhibits an example of this situation. It is dead. White gave up this chain, although the envelopment was not carried through, because there was no way to prevent being enclosed. Plate 7 diagrams (d) and (e) as well as Plate 8 diagrams (b)-(d) show the phases that would have to be carried through in order to complete the enclosure. The outer enclosure is taken therein as already completed. At this juncture, shown in Plate 7 diagram (d), Black has strategically added three additional stones to the already existing inner one shown in Plate 4 and at the next move could complete the inner enclosure and take away the White chain. Therefore White, if he wishes to attempt to stay alive, must now take the four Black stones by placing his own on the still free point. This moment of play is shown in Plate 7 diagram (e), but displaced to the right 90° just as Plate 7 diagram (d) in contrast with the situation in Plate 4 has been so shifted in presentation. Now if it were open to White to play a stone immediately, the situation would be saved in that White could occupy the middle of the four free points, as Plate 8 diagram (a) shows. Black could no longer effect an enclosure from within because his stones in each of the three free places would be immediately enclosed on four sides, and thus would be dead and could be removed from the board. Therefore Black plays at once upon this point and must place two other stones strategically next to it before White can take them with the next play. See Plate 8 diagram (b). White now takes with the result shown in Plate 8 diagram (c) and the situation is comparable to Plate 8 diagram (a). If Black does not now occupy the middle point, White could occupy it and thus be saved. So Black occupies that point and adds another stone, as shown in Plate 8 diagram (d). White captures again and in two more moves, about the course of which there can be no doubt, is dead.

There are no rules beyond the ones already exhibited. Presented again synoptically, the rules are as follows:[18]

1. The players one after another place a stone on any chosen point of the board.

2. Any one or more stones, surrounded on all sides by those of an opponent, are taken at once. If they are not tightly surrounded, but could be certainly, then they are not taken until the end of the game.

3. A stone that has taken one and only one stone cannot be re-taken earlier than the second play following.*

4. The game is over when the completed chains of White and Black stones are in contact, with no intermediary space.

5. That player is the winner whose chains enclose the greater number of free points. At the count, captured stones are placed in the opponent's field.

[6. *When opposing chains each having one or no eyes are so intertwined that neither player can capture his opponent's stones by playing first, neither player is required to make a play which will change the situation, both chains are deemed to be*

*[This situation is called *Ko*. See Plate 6. *Eds.*]

[40]

alive, and the unoccupied points between the two chains are not counted.] *

[*7. The formation known as "bent-four" in the corner as shown in Plate 9 is unconditionally dead.*]

[*8. The stronger player may be handicapped by allowing the weaker player to place one or more stones on his first play. A handicap of one stone is nothing more than the right to play first on any point. Plates 10 to 17 show the placing of handicap stones up to nine. A handicap is increased or decreased as the case may be whenever the same player wins three consecutive games against the same opponent with any given handicap.*]

*[This situation is called *Seki*. See Plate 28. *Eds.*]

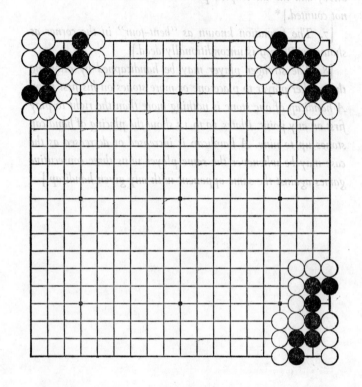

Plate 9

Bent-four in the corner. (Black is dead in each example.)

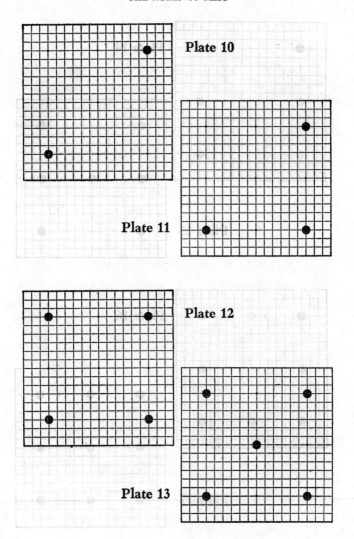

Plate 10

Plate 11

Plate 12

Plate 13

[43]

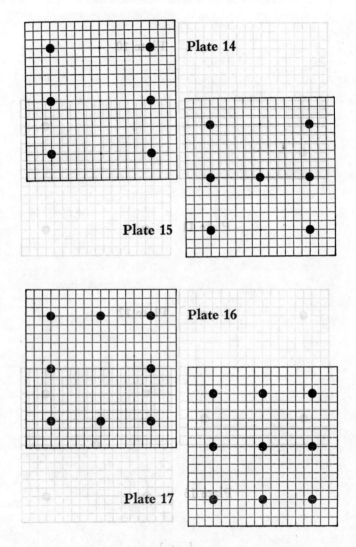

Plate 14

Plate 15

Plate 16

Plate 17

IV

Illustrative Games

COMMENT ON STYLES OF ANNOTATION

PLATE 18 gives an example of the Japanese way of representing a game of *Go*. It is the complete diagram of a finished game. The number on each stone signifies the order of the play in which the stone referred to was placed on the board. But a diagram of this kind cannot reflect all that happens at each play. When a stone has been taken, another is often put in its place; for example, in the case of *Ko* often several stones may be placed eventually at the same spot, each eventually to be re-taken. In a case of this sort a notation referring to it is placed in the margin of the diagram, as, "63 takes in *Ko*." After a certain amount of practice one is not in doubt about where the point is to which "63" belongs though its intersection on the board is not indicated by the notation. Still, although such a diagram with the required marginal notations gives the essentials, this style of presentation is not easy to follow except on the basis of much more than a slight amount of exercise. An inexperienced person is apt to lose a good deal of time while looking for the whereabouts of the point on the board corresponding to the notation.

The Japanese also have another device for exhibiting games which, however, they only apply if they are presenting an analysis of a game of *Go*. They then designate the horizontal lines from bottom to top with numbers 1 to 19 and the vertical lines from right to left likewise with the numbers 1 to 19.[19] For example, Stone 79 on Plate 18 is 5 vertical lines left and 2 horizontal lines up, Stone 81 is 6 vertical lines left and 2 horizontal lines up, and Stone 154 is 17 vertical lines left and 19 horizontal lines up.

But for Western readers it is much better to transfer the international style of chess annotation to *Go*. Because of the fact that in chess the letters run only from A to H and the numbers from 1 to 8, an addition must be made in *Go* of letters through T [except I] and of numbers through 19, to provide for the greater magnitude of the board. Plate 18 shows this co-ordination of letters and numbers, and since in principle it is exactly like the system of annotation in chess it is intelligible without further elucidation.

GAMES

Game I: White: Murase Shuho, *Seventh Rank*

Black: Uchigaki Sutekichi, *Fifth Rank*

(Played on the 21st of March, 1880)   PLATE 18

1. As first steps in the opening game one should occupy the corners and margins as soon as possible, because there are located the positions easiest to occupy that at once both cannot be cut off and also enclose territory. From these elementary situations, the player should work toward the center, an approach repeated in every game.

3. In order to secure one of the still free corners, there remains a choice among seven points. In the corner D4, for example, points D3, D4, D5, C4, C5, E3, E4 are equal. But it would be wrong to take C3 or E5. The territory assured by C3 is too small, and after E5 an opponent would follow with D4, by which E5 would be cut off from the margin. Of the remaining plays D3 and C4 are the safest and most frequently played. Formerly, E4 and D5 were preferred but now D3 and C4. E3 and C5 are only seldom used. The same expedients are valid for the points symmetrical with the above in the other three corners.

4. The attack could also begin at P16.

6. Corresponding to White 4, this play should have been at R5 or Q5. But White goes to Q6, because if he plays R5, Black will follow with R10 or R9, then White

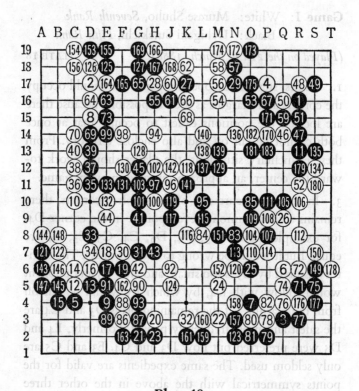

Plate 18

with P5 and Black with O4, the result being that White would gain nothing, but Black two positions, one on lines 3 and 4 from O—Q and another on line R.

7. A beginner would have replied to Q6 with either Q5 or R5. He would attack his opponent at close quarters immediately, because he is not able to grasp the entire field in a single intuitive moment. Such a player's center of attention is absorbed by his opponent's last play. If two beginners are playing together, the battle meanders tediously from some corner out over the whole board, and one side of the board is entirely filled with stones while the other is completely bare. This is a sure symptom of bad playing. At first, good players distribute their stones strategically over the board as much as possible and avoid any close conflict.

8. Position D15—D17 is very strong and a favorite. (Here, of course, and for similar assertions, one should understand that the same holds for all symmetrical situations on the board, of which there are eight in all; *e.g.* C16—E16, Q3—Q5, etc.). As soon as a player thus takes up a position, his opponent at the next play often takes up an equivalent one to equalize in turn the advantage gained by his opponent, like castling in chess.

10. If White does not now occupy C10, the following may occur:

B	W
C10	C7
C13	E7

and Black has the advantage, since the White stones at C7—E7 can thus make an enclosure with only one eye (in Japanese *Me*) on the margin of the board and must later seek connection with another chain. By pressure at such a tender spot, an opponent may gain much territory.

11. Instead of taking the safe place on line R, Black should have fallen on White P17 with L17, whereby Black would have gained positions on line 17 and on line R.

12. White sees that Black is playing too cautiously and challenges him by a clever though premature attack that serves to characterize the whole game.

20. Immediately after Black's answer White will occupy the space on the right or left of H3.

21. Very cautiously played. K3 would have been better. Then in order to save H3, White would either have played H5, whereupon Black would have followed with F7, White E8, Black K5; or White would have answered with K4.

22. Two stones, mutually supporting one another on the board and which are intended to form a position, cannot be more than two points apart, as R13—R16. If they are properly placed in this way, the opponent cannot cut them apart. Consider the following continuations:

B	W
R13 and R16	R14
S14	R15

S15	Q16
R17	Q13
then R12	Q12
or Q14	Q15
R12	P14*

or

R13 and R16	R14
S14	S13
R15	R12
Q14*	S12

or

R13 and R16	R14
S14	S15
R15	S13
Q14*	T14

Bad for White.

[* = takes the stone which is in check. *Eds.*]

Though making no eyes for himself by means of moves 20 and 22, White must fill territory that otherwise would fall to Black.

23. The only proper answer would have been K3, whereby White 20 and 22 would have been separated.

24. Tries to effect a connection with White 6; prevented by Black 25. It is most important to prevent an opponent's emplacements of stones, constructed on the edge, from being joined, in order to keep them weak and thus keeping him on the defensive answering threats or else suffering harm. The player who has the Upperhand*

*[See p. 59, Game II, Play 19. *Eds.*]

most of the time in the game usually comes out the victor.

26. This play is essential, if Black is not to be given the entire right side.

27. Good players are all of the opinion that this play 27 should have gone to L17, not to K17; which is not easy to understand because K17 can be supported on both sides by G17 and N17. L17 is better, because it is not merely a question of occupying a position but more especially of killing White 4. Later, K17 actually will be taken by White.

28. Gives up White 4 at P17. After Black 29 at N17, White 4 could still escape through P15, but to give it up would gain more territory elsewhere than would be lost there by a sacrifice. A dodge much beloved by strong players is that of apparently giving up a position to a weaker opponent, but this is not done without making provision to bring the position back to life later, or so that eventually it can be made to enclose a part of the weaker adversary's chains. An abandoned position often comes to life if the weaker player allows his enclosing chain to be itself enclosed in turn and taken before he can complete his enclosing of the abandoned position.

32. Perhaps it would have been better to go to G8. Then if Black were to follow at H7 White could retort at G10, and then the White position on line D would be quite important. H3, to be sure, would be given up, but not M3—M5. Since 32 K3 is purely defensive, Black wins the

attack and significantly reduces the White territory around line D.

42. Were it not for this move dividing the two Black emplacements, Black would now be overwhelming.

44. This joins the two parts of the White formation which Black 33 threatened to separate. The Upperhand remains with White because Black cannot allow his position to be broken up by means of F10.

52. The beginner will wonder why 52 Q15 does not follow 51 R15. This is because 53 R10, 54 R9 would then be played, which would put White at a great disadvantage. White 46—52 are part of a carefully planned strategy by White. As long as White 4 was alone Black could ignore it. Therefore White augments it by means of White 48 and White 50. Black must accept this sacrifice since if he does not Black 27—29 are in danger. But this series of plays gives White the area around Black 27 and allows him to enlarge his position on line Q with this move.

With move 53 Black goes on with the capture of White 4, 48 and 50, and White captures Black 27 with White 54.

55. White does not heed this because Black must answer to moves 56 and 58 in order not to lose 29—53.

67. Either this play must be made or else the following will happen:

B	W
—	P16
P15	O15
N15	N16
O17	O14

P18 with White having the advantage.

73. Black must now make every effort to occupy this point because if he does not, White will penetrate from there deep into his position. He goes indeed first, however, at his 71st move to R5 because White must follow there, and then to 73, because there he loses Upperhand. Continuing Black could have occupied S5 after R5 and before E15, since White would have followed with S6; for otherwise the following continuation would result:

B	W
S5	E15
S6	S7
S8	T7
R8	R7

Q8 and the White position is destroyed.

Because Black played too hastily at E15 and did not seize S5 earlier, White can destroy the Black position by moves 74—82.

Murase Shuho considers White 74 a bad move; S5 would have been better, and the following would result:

B	W
E15	S5
R4	S4

or alternatively if Black plays

	S4	then	R4
	Q5		S3
	R3		T4*
	S2		

Murase also regards plays 76—82 as being bad for White because nothing was particularly accomplished through the separation of O4—O6, since the result of this series of moves is that the remaining Black stones near the margin are strengthened and can no longer be killed.

91. Black must make this play, because otherwise E6—F6 will die by means of:

B	W
—	E5
F5*	E5*

93. This protects H2, G2, G3. This can be done most simply by a play at F2, but G4 is worth six more points, because F3—F4 are to be regarded as taken.

With the play from White 94 on, the territory in the center is filled up, Black and White coming out more or less evenly.

121. A move worth noticing.

152. Not at M7 because that would entail the loss of K8—L8.

183. This is as far as the game was reproduced in the magazine on *Go* published by Murase Shuho. A good player may now foresee the result, though it may take some effort. Black has won by 5 points. As I [Korschelt]

see it, the game would have proceeded thus [*numbering added by the Editors*]:

	184. T5	207. F16	208. J2
185. T4	186. T7	209. J1	210. J3
187. S3	188. G15	211. M7	212. L7
189. G16	190. J8	213. H4	214. J4
191. H8	192. N13	215. N15	216. K9
193. N12	194. M14	217. K10	218. M2
195. J7	196. K7	219. M1	220. Q13
197. F8	198. E8	221. M15	222. L15
199. D10	200. D9	223. F9	224. Q12
201. J15	202. J14	225. P12	226. T13
203. J19*	204. K19	227. T14	228. T12
205. Q11	206. F15	229. H19	

The stones that remain to be played are useless *(Dame)*. By playing these no eyes can be either won or lost, and mostly it makes no difference whether they are placed by Black or White.*

	230. N16	235. H5	236. H6
231. O15	232. E13	237. F10	238. H15
233. E12	234. F13		

B 64 points

W 59 points

This agrees incidentally with Murase's result. Mostly one would not gain more than one eye or so more; for, it is very difficult to find the best plays and, even more so, the best play sequences.

*[This must be qualified. *Eds.*]

[Consecutive plays listed by the Editors]

Black	White		
1. R16	2. D17	61. J16	62. K18
3. Q3	4. P17	63. E16	64. D16
5. C4	6. Q6	65. G17	66. K16
7. O4	8. D15	67. P16	68. K15
9. E4	10. C10	69. D14	70. C14
11. R13	12. C5	71. R5	72. R6
13. D5	14. C6	73. E15	74. Q5
15. B4	16. D6	75. S5	76. Q4
17. E6	18. E7	77. R3	78. P3
19. F6	20. H3	79. P2	80. O3
21. G2	22. M3	81. O2	82. P4
23. H2	24. M5	83. N8	84. L8
25. O6	26. Q9	85. O10	86. F3
27. K17	28. H17	87. G3	88. F4
29. N17	30. F7	89. E3	90. G5
31. G7	32. K3	91. E5	92. J6
33. D8	34. D7	93. G4	94. H14
35. D11	36. C11	95. L10	96. J11
37. D12	38. C12	97. H11	98. F14
39. D13	40. C13	99. E14	100. H10
41. G9	42. G6	101. G10	102. H12
43. H7	44. E9	103. G11	104. O8
45. G12	46. Q14	105. Q10	106. R10
47. R14	48. R17	107. P8	108. P9
49. S17	50. Q16	109. O9	110. O7
51. R15	52. R11	111. P10	112. R8
53. O16	54. M16	113. N7	114. P7
55. H16	56. M17	115. L9	116. K8
57. N18	58. M18	117. J9	118. K12
59. Q15	60. J17	119. J10	120. N6
		121. A7	122. B7

123. N2	*124.* J5	*155.* E19	*156.* C18
125. E18	*126.* D18	*157.* N3	*158.* N4
127. G18	*128.* G13	*159.* L2	*160.* L3
129. M12	*130.* F12	*161.* K2	*162.* F5
131. F11	*132.* E10	*163.* F2	*164.* E17
133. E11	*134.* S12	*165.* F17	*166.* H19
135. S13	*136.* N14	*167.* H18	*168.* J18
137. L12	*138.* L13	*169.* G19	*170.* P14
139. M13	*140.* L14	*171.* P15	*172.* N19
141. K11	*142.* J12	*173.* O19	*174.* M19
143. A6	*144.* A8	*175.* O17	*176.* R4
145. B5	*146.* B6	*177.* S4	*178.* T6
147. A5	*148.* B8	*179.* R12	*180.* S11
149. S6	*150.* S7	*181.* O13	*182.* O14
151. M8	*152.* M6	*183.* P13	
153. D19	*154.* C19		

Game II: White: Inouye Inseki

Black: Yasui Shintetsu   PLATE 19

(Played on the 20th of December, 1835. From a Japanese work entitled KACHI SEI KYOKU*)*

6.   Just as good as the already known D15 in Game I.

7.   In the given situation this may be the best play. The firm position Q3—Q5 protects equally the outposts C4 and R16.

18.   Q14 is now beyond help; for—

B	W
Q13	P14
O14	P13

P12   O13
N13   O12
O11 etc.

If White could have placed a stone on the line of retreat of Q14—perhaps at E3, which Black would have been forced to answer—then rescue would have been possible by means of P14 etc.

19.   S14 would have been decidedly better, since it is a play (called *Sente* by the Japanese) known as the Upperhand: a play to which the opponent must either answer or else suffer a severe loss.[*] To Black's S14 White must answer with S16 in order not to lose R15—S15 whereby Black would gain an absolutely safe position and the corner, which is worth about fourteen points. Then perhaps White S16 might be answered by Black at R12 and thus Black would obtain a safe position.

24.   This is an analogue of White 8, but does not push forward so much because of Black 23.

32.   White has built a strong wall on line D and left Black much territory, to be able to occupy L3. If the play at L3 had followed immediately upon Black 23 at J3, then either L3 or E3 would have been greatly endangered.

41.   Black compels White to take this stone in order to make his own escape.

_____

*[The reader should note that here Upperhand (*Sente*) is both defined and exemplified. *Eds*.]

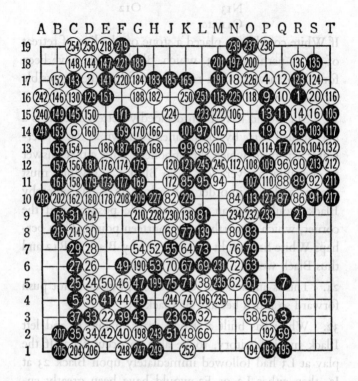

Plate 19

78 J7 Connects; 93 R10 Connects; *Ko* 119 P12, 122, 125, 128, 131; 133 Q14 Connects; *Ko* 134 P13, 137, 140, 142 P12 Connects; *Ko* 216 S11, 253, 255 S11 Connects.

49. Upperhand.

56. Similar to Game I, White 12.

64. An interesting attack that determines the course of the play for some time. Black 65 J8 would mean the sacrifice of the position on G—J (26 points), but would offer an opportunity for a bold attack. With 65 J6 Black would scarcely survive.

65. Upperhand. White must reply or else not retain eyes in that position.

71. Avoids *Ko* but still establishes connection.

74. Played for same reason as White 66.

86. Now the mistake of Black 19 begins to exact its revenge.

93. Q12 should no doubt be better, or at least safer; for it effects a connection by way of P11 after White has taken. If White does not take, but plays at P11, his stones at the margin will die.

94. A play that separates P14 from K11 and is simultaneously Upperhand with regard to the Black stones on line K; for, if Black does not retort, then these stones would be cut off by White at K10. Moves 98, 100, 102 conclusively isolate the Black stones around P14.

107. It is certain that either the eight Black or else the five White stones must die; and on this option depends victory, since a matter of forty points is involved.

142. White would have had another *Ko* threat at M10.

152. Note well the plays in sequence 143—152, since they occur frequently.

159. Upperhand.

163. Not to be played at B10, so that the Upperhand can be kept and without losing too many points.

164. Better go to K17.

198. Upperhand. Threatens the three Black stones on lines J and K.

208. C8 should have been played first.

White has won by 7 points.

[Consecutive plays listed by the Editors]

Black	White		
1. R16	2. D17	31. C9	32. L3
3. Q3	4. P17	33. D3	34. D2
5. C4	6. C14	35. C2	36. D4
7. Q5	8. Q14	37. C3	38. L5
9. P16	10. Q16	39. F3	40. F2
11. Q15	12. Q17	41. E4	42. E2
13. P15	14. R15	43. G3	44. F4
15. R14	16. S15	45. G4	46. F5
17. Q13	18. N17	47. G5	48. K2
19. P14*	20. S16	49. F6	50. E5*
21. R9	22. E3	51. J2	52. H7
23. J3	24. D5	53. H6	54. G7
25. C5	26. D6	55. J7	56. P3
27. C6	28. D7	57. P4	58. O3
29. C7	30. D8	59. Q2	60. O4
		61. O5	62. N5

63. O6	64. K7	123. R17	124. S17
65. K3	66. L2	125. P12 *Ko*	126. R13
67. K6	68. J8	127. P10	128. P13 *Ko*
69. L6	70. J6*	129. D16	130. C16
71. K5	72. N6	131. P12 *Ko*	132. T13
73. L7	74. K4	133. Q14	134. P13 *Ko*
75. J5	76. N7	Connects	
77. K8	78. J7	135. S18	136. R18*
	Connects	137. P12 *Ko*	138. K9
79. O7	80. N8	139. L8	140. P13 *Ko*
81. L9	82. J10	141. E17	142. P12
83. O8	84. N10		Connects
85. K11	86. R10	143. C17	144. D18
87. Q10	88. Q11	145. C15	146. B16
89. R11	90. R12	147. E18	148. C18
91. S10*	92. S11	149. B15	150. D15
93. R10	94. M11	151. E16	152. B17*
Connects		153. B14	154. C13
95. L11	96. Q12	155. B13	156. C12
97. L14	98. L13	157. B12	158. C11
99. K13	100. M13	159. F14	160. D14
101. K14	102. M14	161. B11	162. C10
103. S14	104. S13	163. B9	164. D9
105. T15	106. N15	165. K17	166. H14
107. O11	108. O12	167. G13	168. H13
109. P12	110. P11	169. G11	170. G14
111. O13	112. N12	171. F15	172. J11
113. O10	114. P13*	173. E11	174. F12
115. M16	116. T16	175. G12	176. E12
117. T14	118. O16	177. F11	178. E10
119. P12 *Ko*	120. J12	179. D11	180. D10
121. K12	122. P13 *Ko*	181. D12	182. H16

183. H17	184. G17	221. F18	222. M15
185. J17	186. E13	223. L15	224. J15
187. F13	188. G16	225. N16	226. O17
189. G18	190. G6	227. H10	228. H9
191. M17	192. P2	229. K10	230. J9
193. P1	194. O1	231. M6	232. O9
195. Q1	196. L4	233. P9	234. N9
197. N18	198. G2	235. M5	236. M4
199. H5	200. O18	237. O19	238. P19
201. M18	202. B10	239. N19	240. A15
203. A10	204. C1	241. A14	242. A16
205. B1	206. D1	243. H2	244. J4
207. B2	208. F10	245. L12	246. M12
209. G10	210. G9	247. G1	248. F1
211. T11	212. T12	249. H1	250. K16
213. S12*	214. C8	251. L16	252. K1
215. B8	216. S11 Ko	253. S12 Ko	254. C19
217. T10	218. E19	255. S11	256. D19
219. F19	220. F17	Connects	

Game III: White: Inouye Inseki

Black: Hon-In-Bo Sanchi PLATE 20

(Played on the 20th of May and the 17th and 25th of June, 1839)

5. Players today would regard the position C4—E3 as excessively petty and circumspect. F4 or F3 are better.

7. That Black does not retort here to the attack at 6 promises a brisk game.

14-26. These moves are analogues of 8—20 in Game II. Only 24 (Game II White 18) is further toward the center, made possible by White G17 (while in Game II White stood at too great a distance on D17).

25. This should be evaluated as Black 19 in Game II was, but less adversely, because connections are possible at E9 and F15.

32. Black has a sure position in prospect with C17 and it is up to White to seize it as soon as possible.

43. Under favorable conditions Black can now live. B15 and A14 and C14 would be the eyes.

44. Since White is strengthened on line 11, an attack on C9—E9 can be launched and conjointly with this Black territory can be disrupted.

52. This is a clever play, which Black would have done much better to answer with 53 H4. The play at 54 is pregnant with implications. White backs up 52 by means of 56, thereby compelling or seducing Black into taking them both. This results in White's being pushed away from this position by Black and so upward where he has an opportunity for the decisive plays 66 and 68. Play 66 opens the rear line of defense on line 8 and drastically threatens Black on line 9. Play 68 is aimed against Black on lines 9 and 15, and has about the same force as "check" in chess.*

---

*[The situation called *Atari* is more nearly comparable to "check." See for example Plate 7, diagrams (a) and (d), p. 36. *Eds.*]

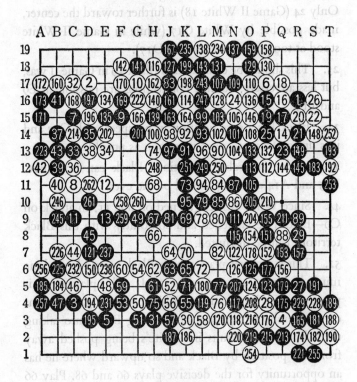

Plate 20

147 Q14 Connects; *Ko* 200 D15, 203, 206, 209, 212, 217 D14, 218 D16 Connects; *Ko* 224 C14, 227, 230, 233, 236, 239; 240 M19, 241 L19*; *Ko* 242 C14, 244 D14 Connects.

74. White perhaps should play first L4 or L5, then H13, or, in fact, H15, which would be considerably better.

81. Otherwise White by means of J10 will split apart Black's H9 and K11.

107. Play O14 would be wrong. For White K16 would follow, and White, though sacrificing L11—M11, would still win four of Black's stones and enough territory to make victory certain. Black must, therefore, develop the four stones into an emplacement and, as the matter stands, has now three weak places while White is safe overall. Now follows an interesting struggle.

115. Very good.

136. Would probably go better after L16.

141. A sacrifice in order to consolidate both of the Black positions.

144. From here on White begins to make use of Black's faulty play 25. Now is the suitable time to occupy 150 D6, a play worth twenty-four points; and Black is further forced to play 151 P8 in order to protect his position on line 9, whereby the Upperhand is lost until play 160. Black now has some 59 points and White 62.

164. If Black, whose turn it is, protects—which is very necessary—the connection between lines D and L by means of G14, White S4 will follow, a play yielding six points, and White would probably win by some nine points. Accordingly, Black must play R3, but will still suffer in this situation because 166 G15 is Upperhand in

relation to the position on line L. Play 168 by means of J19 would destroy the position on line L.

173. The Black stones on line B could be saved by means of D15, otherwise White can induce a *Ko* by means of D15, which might spell defeat for Black. Black must let the play happen, though, and retort to White's R2.

180. A play that is more important than it seems. It simultaneously saves L9—M9.

183. S13 would be altogether bad. Play 183 ought to impede White T13.

184. White still retains the superior stance. If Black plays 185 at D15, White will gain the Upperhand and win by eight points.

185. Too little—worth, say, four or six points, that White yields in order to keep Upperhand.

192. Furnishes a point to be used for the ensuing *Ko*.

214. Black offers more chances for *Ko* than White because White through 202 E14 secured play 214 C14 and, accordingly, 218 D16 also. Thereby the first row of fortifications is lost. There is still a prospect for victory by means of the occupancy by Black of A13 and C14.

243. White has no further *Ko* threats. Therefore White must allow Black to keep the three stones L15. Move 136 could have killed these stones, if a play had

been made to L16, but then the attack, introduced at move 144, would have been impossible.

White has won by 8 points.

[*Consecutive plays listed by the Editors*]

Black	White		
1. R16	*2.* D17	*49.* G9	*50.* G4
3. C4	*4.* Q3	*51.* G3	*52.* J5
5. E3	*6.* P17	*53.* F4	*54.* G6
7. C15	*8.* C11	*55.* K4	*56.* J4
9. F15	*10.* G17	*57.* J3	*58.* L3
11. C9	*12.* E11	*59.* F5	*60.* F6
13. E9	*14.* Q14	*61.* H5	*62.* H6
15. P16	*16.* Q16	*63.* J6	*64.* J7
17. Q15	*18.* Q17	*65.* K6	*66.* H8
19. P15	*20.* R15	*67.* H9	*68.* H11
21. R14	*22.* S15	*69.* K9	*70.* K7
23. Q13	*24.* N16	*71.* K5	*72.* L6
25. P14*	*26.* S16	*73.* K11	*74.* H13
27. R5	*28.* P4	*75.* H4*	*76.* M4
29. R8	*30.* K3	*77.* M5	*78.* L9
31. H3	*32.* C17	*79.* L10	*80.* M9
33. C13	*34.* E13	*81.* J9	*82.* M7
35. D14	*36.* C12	*83.* J17	*84.* M11
37. B14	*38.* D13	*85.* M10	*86.* N10
39. B12	*40.* B11	*87.* N11	*88.* Q8
41. B16	*42.* A12	*89.* R9	*90.* M13
43. B13	*44.* C7	*91.* K13	*92.* K14
45. D8	*46.* C5	*93.* L14	*94.* L11
47. B4	*48.* E5	*95.* K10	*96.* L13
		97. J13	*98.* J14

99. L15	100. H14	161. J16	162. H17
101. N14	102. M14	163. J15	164. K15
103. M15	104. N13	165. R3	166. G15
105. O11	106. N15	167. J19	168. C16
107. M17	108. O14*	169. F16	170. F17
109. N17	110. O17	171. A15	172. A17
111. N9	112. P12	173. A16	174. R2
113. O12	114. K16	175. Q4	176. P3
115. N8	116. H18	177. P6	178. O7
117. N4	118. N3	179. Q5	180. L5
119. L4	120. M3	181. S3	182. S2
121. D7	122. N7	183. S12	184. B5
123. P5	124. O5	185. A5	186. K2
125. O6	126. N6	187. J2	188. T3
127. J18	128. M16	189. T4	190. T2
129. O18	130. P18	191. S5	192. T12
131. M18	132. P13	193. T13	194. D4
133. O13	134. E16	195. D3	196. D15
135. E15	136. O16	197. D16*	198. K17
137. N19	138. L19	199. K18	200. D15 Ko
139. H15	140. H16	201. G14	202. E14
141. G18	142. F18	203. D16 Ko	204. O9
143. L18	144. Q12	205. O10*	206. D15 Ko
145. R12	146. O15	207. N5	208. O4
147. Q14	148. S14	209. D16 Ko	210. P10
Connects		211. Q9*	212. D15 Ko
149. R13	150. D6	213. Q2	214. C14*
151. P8	152. P7	215. P2	216. O3
153. Q7	154. O8	217. D14 Ko	218. D16
155. P9	156. Q6		Connects
157. R7	158. P19	219. O2	220. N2
159. O19	160. B17	221. R1	222. G16

223. A13	224. C14 Ko	243. L17	244. D14
225. B6	226. B7		Connects
227. D14 Ko	228. S4	245. B9	246. B10
229. R4*	230. C14 Ko	247. L16	248. H12
231. E4	232. C6	249. L12	250. M12
233. D14 Ko	234. M19	251. K12	252. T14
235. K19*	236. C14 Ko	253. T11*	254. O1
237. E7	238. E6	255. S1	256. A6*
239. D14 Ko	240. M19	257. A4	258. F10
241. L19*	242. C14 Ko	259. F9	260. G10
		261. D10	262. D11

Game IV: White: Inouye Inseki

          Black: Hon-In-Bo Sanchi   PLATE 21

(Played on the 29th of May, the 25th of June, and the 2nd and 17th of July, 1871)

10—15. Turns up frequently.

16 and 18. Attack too soon and allow Black to make a strong counterattack.

33. Would be perhaps better at O12 which would tend to protect a considerable territory for Black.

52. To S3, otherwise White will be taken there. Not S4, then Black goes to S2 and kills White in spite of it.

53. Black assumes obviously that White will retort with G5 or G6 and that then he can play J8 and force White toward line A. But White quite properly answers with J8 and builds up a good array from 54 to 58.

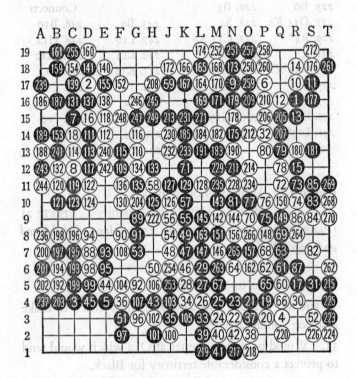

Plate 21

Ko 158 D17; 216 H11*; *Ko* 221 G11, 227 H11 Connects;
256 D18 Connects; 267 M7 Connects.

59. O12 would be better. At White K17, Black plays G17, White then K15 and there ensues, certainly, a difficult but not at all hopeless struggle, in that Black can so maneuver that he gains a position between lines F and N on line 16, whereby, though, the considerable territory at right is mostly lost.

76. This is wrong. It was essential to move to O10, through which play all of White's stones around line O would have been saved.

89—95. Cannot possibly be good. They only go to show, what one could have seen earlier, that stone 53, which was a mistaken play, should have been given up without further ado. Black must begin with C15 and advance from F12, H12 and E11 forwards. Thus, perhaps, he can establish an extensive position between lines G and L and 12 and 19 as well as bring a lesser position in the left upper corner up to strength.

108. With this play the stones played by Black from moves 89—95 are killed and White appears equally situated with Black.

109. This move, which should have been made at the time of play 89 or 91, now comes too late. Instead of helping it will imprison, along with itself, all stones that come to its assistance, although it does make possible the construction of the modest position in the left corner and the rescue of G7—G10. The sacrifice is just about as great

as the accomplished gain. And so 109 G13 would have been better.

142. An effort conceived in the hope of coaxing the opponent into making an error.

152. In order not to allow line E to be breached E17 suffices, especially since it is Upperhand in relation to B18; at the same time the play should be brought forward towards the right.

157 and 163. Black must retort in such wise that his right side is not enveloped.

239—243. An adroit raid which bags three points for Black.

Black and White are equal.

[Consecutive plays listed by the Editors]

Black	White		
1. R16	2. D17	25. M4	26. L4
3. C4	4. Q3	27. L5	28. K5
5. E4	6. P17	29. L6	30. R4
7. C15	8. C12	31. S5	32. P14
9. N17	10. R17	33. L3	34. K4
11. S17	12. Q16	35. J3	36. F4
13. R15	14. R18	37. O3	38. O2
15. R12	16. D15	39. L2	40. M2
17. R5	18. C14	41. M1	42. N2
19. P4	20. P3	43. H4	44. E5
21. O4	22. N3	45. D4	46. K6
23. N4	24. M3	47. K7	48. J7
		49. K8	50. H6

51. F3	52. S3	115. F13	116. G14
53. G7	54. J8	117. D12	118. E15
55. K9	56. J9	119. C11	120. B11
57. K10	58. H11	121. B10	122. D11
59. J17	60. Q5	123. C10	124. D10
61. Q6	62. P6	125. H10	126. J10
63. Q7	64. N6	127. J11	128. L11
65. P5	66. Q4	129. K11	130. F10
67. M5	68. P7	131. C16	132. B12
69. Q8	70. O9	133. H12	134. G12
71. K12	72. Q11	135. G11*	136. F11
73. R11	74. R10	137. D16	138. E16
75. P9	76. P10	139. C17	140. E18
77. O10	78. Q12	141. D18	142. M9
79. Q13	80. P13	143. M10	144. N9
81. N10	82. S7	145. L9	146. M7
83. S10	84. S9	147. L7	148. P8
85. S11	86. R9	149. Q9	150. Q10
87. R6	88. D7	151. M8	152. F17
89. G9	90. F8	153. B14	154. C18
91. G8	92. G5	155. E17*	156. N8
93. E7	94. D8	157. O7	158. D17 *Ko*
95. E6	96. G3	159. B18	160. D19*
97. F2	98. D6	161. B19	162. O6
99. D5	100. J2	163. L8	164. L17
101. H2	102. H3	165. L18	166. K18
103. J4	104. F5	167. K17	168. M18
105. K3	106. H5	169. L16	170. M17
107. G4	108. F7	171. M16	172. J18
109. F12	110. G13	173. N18	174. L19*
111. D14	112. E14	175. N14	176. S18
113. D13	114. C13	177. S16	178. N15

179. N16	180. R13	229. M12	230. J14
181. S13	182. M14	231. K15	232. J13
183. M13	184. L14	233. K13	234. O11
185. K14	186. A16	235. M11	236. A8
187. B16	188. A13	237. A4	238. A6
189. A14	190. N13	239. A17	240. E13
191. L13	192. B5	241. B13	242. E12*
193. C6	194. B6	243. A12*	244. A11
195. C7	196. C8	245. H16	246. G16
197. B7	198. B8	247. G15	248. F15
199. C5	200. A7	249. H15	250. O18
201. A6	202. A5*	251. N19	252. M19
203. B4	204. G10	253. J5	254. J6
205. Q15	206. P15	255. C19	256. D18
207. Q14	208. H17		Connects
209. O16	210. P16	257. O19	258. P19
211. N12	212. O14*	259. O17	260. P18
213. J15	214. O12	261. T18	262. T6
215. T5	216. H11*	263. M6	264. R8
217. N1	218. O1	265. N7*	266. O8
219. L1	220. Q2	267. M7	268. T10
221. G11 Ko	222. H9	Connects	
223. T3	224. T2	269. T11	270. T9
225. T4	226. S2	271. L15	272. S19
227. H11	228. N11		
Connects			

Game V: White: Yasui Shintetsu
         Black: Ito Tokube   **PLATE 22**
(Played on the 26th of May, 1835)

18. Another move alongside P17 or perhaps at O15

should have been played prior to this in order to insure a position which would make possible the rear defense of C15—F15. With 18 and 20 White gives Upperhand away and Black exploits this in a capital manner by means of 21 to 29.

30. Now, in fact, White is in a safer position on line 17 but fully exposed on line 15. The extensive territory that White commands on line 3 does not compensate for that.

31. Black opens a rugged attack.

37. Shows quite well the full disadvantage that besets White. Play 37 is now directed against White at line 14 as well as at line 9; more against White at line 14 though. Still White retorts at line 9 because the loss of this position would be the greater of the two.

70. This stone ought to connect up with White's other stones on line 9 later, but play 73 will stop this short.

79. Cuts off White on line 9 from plays 70—72 and, therefore, White seeks to make eyes with 80 C6.

96. Black cannot retort with C15 because then White would live with H14.

99. Even if a retort is not made to 99 R17, White lives; for

B	W
Q19	P19
Q18	K18
J18	N19

but White places 100 at S18 at once in order not to lose

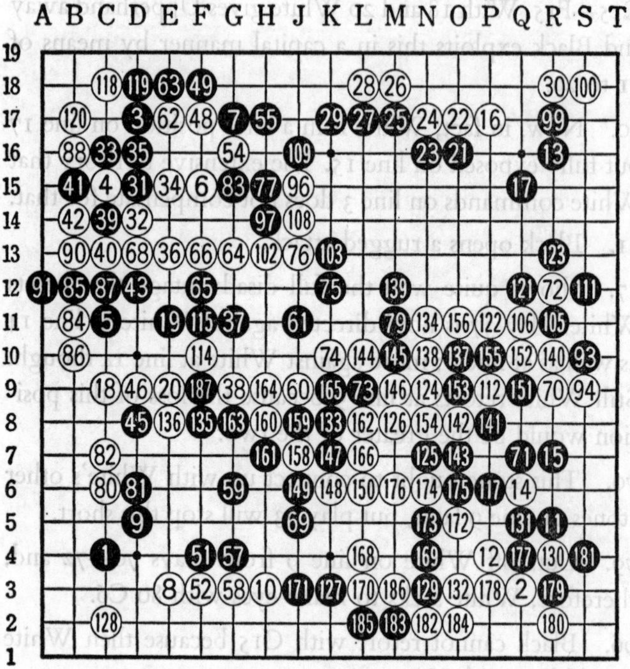

A B C D E F G H J K L M N O P Q R S T

Plate 22

Ko 44 C15, 47, 50, 53, 56, 67, 78, 89, 92, 95, 98, 101, 104, 107, 110, 113, 116; 157 P9 Connects; 167 J7 Connects.

the sixteen points—the worth of this play—and also in order not to leave Black a safe position and because otherwise Black would have two chances for *Ko* at line 18.

118. White saves his position on line 13, and Black's attack is now directed against White's position around Q10 with even greater prospect of success.

127 and 129. Occupy the place where White wanted to seek refuge. This is especially harmful for White because both stones are Upperhand.

135. It is clear that here F9 should follow otherwise three stones would be cut off, which means a difference of twenty points. But White fears Black's B8. One should give thought here to the possibilities of 136 H11.

139—157. Black plays with true finesse.

186. White is saved, but in compensation Black takes six stones with 187, worth twenty points, and also has his position in the lower right corner enlarged during the struggle.

White concedes the game, having lost by 10 points.

[*Consecutive plays listed by the Editors*]

Black	White		
1. C4	2. Q3	11. R5	12. P4
3. D17	4. C15	13. R16	14. Q6
5. C11	6. F15	15. R7	16. P17
7. G17	8. E3	17. Q15	18. C9
9. D5	10. H3	19. E11	20. E9
		21. O16	22. O17

23. N16	24. N17	87. C12	88. B16
25. M17	26. M18	89. C14 Ko	90. B13
27. L17	28. L18	91. A12	92. C15 Ko
29. K17	30. R18	93. S10	94. S9
31. D15	32. D14	95. C14 Ko	96. J15
33. C16	34. E15	97. H14	98. C15 Ko
35. D16	36. E13	99. R17	100. S18
37. G11	38. G9	101. C14 Ko	102. H13
39. C14	40. C13	103. K13	104. C15 Ko
41. B15*	42. B14	105. R11	106. Q11
43. D12	44. C15 Ko	107. C14 Ko	108. J14
45. D8	46. D9	109. J16	110. C15 Ko
47. C14 Ko	48. F17	111. S12	112. P9
49. F18	50. C15 Ko	113. C14 Ko	114. F10
51. F4	52. F3	115. F11	116. C15 Ko
53. C14 Ko	54. G16	117. P6	118. C18
55. H17	56. C15 Ko	119. D18	120. B17
57. G4	58. G3	121. Q12	122. P11
59. G6	60. J9	123. R13*	124. N9
61. J11	62. E17	125. N7	126. M8
63. E18	64. G13	127. K3	128. C2
65. F12	66. F13	129. N3	130. R4
67. C14 Ko	68. D13	131. Q5	132. O3
69. J5	70. R9	133. K8	134. N11
71. Q7	72. R12	135. F8	136. E8
73. L9	74. K10	137. O10	138. N10
75. K12	76. J13	139. M12	140. R10
77. H15	78. C15 Ko	141. P8	142. O8
79. M11	80. C6	143. O7	144. L10
81. D6	82. C7	145. M10	146. M9
83. G15	84. B11	147. K7	148. K6
85. B12	86. B10	149. J6	150. L6

151. Q9	152. Q10	169. N4	170. L3
153. O9	154. N8	171. J3	172. O5
155. P10*	156. O11	173. N5	174. N6
157. P9	158. J7	175. O6	176. M6
Connects		177. Q4	178. P3
159. J8	160. H8	179. R3	180. R2
161. H7*	162. L8	181. S4*	182. N2
163. G8	164. H9	183. M2	184. O2
165. K9	166. L7	185. L2	186. M3
167. J7	168. L4	187. F9	
Connects			

Game VI: White: Yasui Shintetsu

Black: Akahoshi Intetsu　　PLATE 23

(Played on the 30th of April, 1832)

This game has quite exceptional openings.

12. White does not go to Q17 because he expects Black to play C10 or C11, whereupon White would extend C15—D15 to the right. White will then occupy G—L on line 17 and so Black will be forced to push the continuation of C15—D15 further toward the center. White expects during this interval to create a position on the upper edge, and it is the purpose of P17 to lead these stones toward P. If White had played Q17, Black could easily go toward N17 and hinder that intention.

48. As soon as White has to some extent secured his position around T5 and has Upperhand he launches the plan introduced with P17.

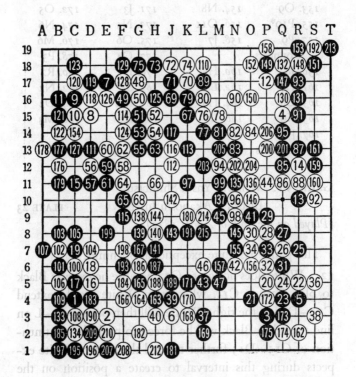

Plate 23

35 Q7 Connects; 194 G5 Connects; 211 D1 Connects.

67. The territory is too extensive. White cannot enclose it. Perhaps 48 H17 would have been better.

70. White finds himself forced to sacrifice the four stones on lines G and H, but the remaining territory will remain that much safer for him.

85. Black apparently expects 86 R11 or Q13.

B	W
Q12	Q13
P12	S11
Q11	O13
N12	O12
O11	R17, etc.

86. But Q11 is better for White. Of course, White with 91 and 93 loses some thirty points and Upperhand, but by enclosing eight Black stones at Q8 he wins likewise thirty points and makes the White stones at lines 5 and 6 permanent, and that is worth several Upperhands.

87. Black is forced to develop the game further along the direction indicated in 86 above. The game now settles down, after White's taking the eight Black stones with 98, in such a way that little opportunity is left for ingenious play. The points yet to be occupied are easily recognized. It is merely a question as to which order of possession is the most advantageous. But since the order of the placements of the positions determines the game, if the difference of free points in the positions is not great, one must concentrate on the apparently insignificant plays with the greatest care.

Black won by 4 points because White with play 48 tried to envelop too much territory. If Black had not played 85 Q12, then his trophy would have been much greater.

*   *   *

This game is excellent for pointing up the general maxim that a player should not undertake to construct the greatest possible territory for himself as White sought to do with Play 48, but, rather, that one ought to allow the least possible territory to one's opponent. The more densely packed the board is at the end and the smaller also the free territory appears the less will be the difference in points during the entire game and the easier it will be to change an unfavorable difference into a favorable one. But also, of course, in conformity with this style of play there is the danger that one who fully has the advantage may lose it—very great, because for the opponent there is no need for any very great effort. This style of play, which one might call "close," underwent its formation at the hands of the two great Go-masters Hon-In-Bo and Yasui, by the former in the first half of the 19th century and by the latter in its middle period. Games II-V and those following belong to this school.

I have chosen them because the problems of this style of play are much less difficult than those presented by the games of the Murase school. The Murase school culti-vates the "wide" style of play in which the opponent does

[84]

not imitate the leading moves so closely, but goes more his own way. With the Hon-In-Bo—Yasui School the chief stress is on the defensive and on the disruption of the opponent's vacant spaces, but with Murase it is on the offensive by means of spreading out the line and on the mobility of the forces, not on an offensive made up of a loose series of skirmishes. Murase's style of play is much more distinguished and splendid, demanding a many times greater investment of effort and alertness, because the relations of the stones on account of their greater range are multiplied many times.

[Consecutive plays listed by the Editors]

Black	White		
1. C4	2. E3	31. Q6	32. P6
3. P3	4. Q15	33. P7*	34. O7
5. R4	6. J3	35. Q7	36. S5
7. E17	8. D15	Connects	
9. C16	10. C15	37. L3	38. S3
11. B16	12. P17	39. J4	40. H3
13. R10	14. R12	41. O9	42. N6
15. C11	16. D5	43. L5	44. P11
17. C5	18. D6	45. M9	46. L6
19. C7	20. P5	47. M5	48. G17
21. O4	22. R5	49. F16	50. G16
23. Q4	24. Q5	51. G15	52. H15
25. R7	26. Q7	53. G14	54. H14
27. Q8	28. P8	55. G13	56. D12
29. P9	30. O8	57. D11	58. F12
		59. E12	60. E13

61. E11	62. F13	125. H16	126. E16
63. H13	64. F11	127. C13	128. F17*
65. F10	66. H11	129. F18	130. Q16
67. K15	68. G10	131. R16	132. Q18
69. J16	70. K17	133. B3	134. C2
71. J17	72. J18	135. N11	136. O11
73. H18	74. K18	137. M10	138. G9
75. G18	76. L15	139. G8	140. H8
77. L14	78. M15	141. H7	142. J10
79. K16	80. L16	143. J8	144. H9
81. M14	82. N14	145. N8	146. O10
83. N13	84. O14	147. Q17	148. R18
85. Q12	86. Q11	149. P18	150. O16
87. R13	88. R11	151. S18	152. O18
89. L17	90. N16	153. R19	154. C14
91. R15	92. S10	155. N7	156. O6
93. R17	94. M12	157. M6	158. P19*
95. Q14	96. N10	159. S12	160. S11
97. K11	98. N9	161. S13	162. R2
99. M11	100. C6	163. H4	164. G4
101. B6	102. B7	165. G5	166. F4
103. B8	104. D7	167. G7	168. K3
105. C8	106. B5	169. L2	170. K4
107. A7*	108. C3	171. K5	172. P4
109. B4	110. L18	173. Q3	174. Q2
111. D13	112. J12	175. P2	176. B12
113. K13	114. F15	177. B13	178. A13
115. F9	116. J13	179. B11	180. K9
117. J14	118. D16	181. J1	182. G2
119. D17	120. C17	183. D4	184. F5
121. B15	122. B14	185. B2	186. G6
123. C18	124. F14	187. H6	188. H5*

189. J5	*190.* D3	*203.* L12	*204.* O12
191. K8	*192.* S19	*205.* M13	*206.* P14
193. F6	*194.* G5	*207.* E1	*208.* F1
	Connects	*209.* D2*	*210.* E2
195. C1	*196.* D1	*211.* D1	*212.* H1
197. B1	*198.* F7		Connects
199. E8	*200.* P13	*213.* T19*	*214.* L9
201. Q13	*202.* N12	*215.* L8	

Game VII: White: Yasui Shintetsu

Black: Mizutani Takuma   PLATE 24

(Played on the 19th of July, 1836)

This game is of interest because of the free mobility with which the players shift about on the board. White, especially, plays a very dashing game.

39. This is outstanding. It provokes the impressive episode 40—52, with the result that White has only a moderately secure position at P4 (also one at D2, but too small), while Black is entrenched at D16 and R16. Everything else is in doubt, though Black has good prospects at the middle of the left edge. From 55 on both players are forced into taking the boldest measures.

100. White's predicament has gradually improved.

110. It is proper for White to secure his position on line G, but it would be better first to get the position at G10 thoroughly in hand. Black is weak there and must reply because he can twice be cut in two at F9.

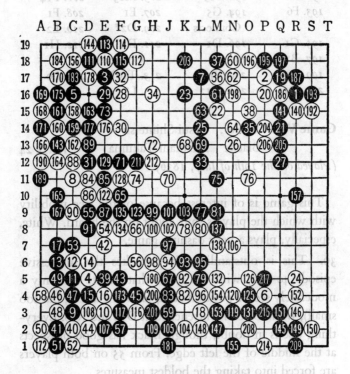

Plate 24

Ko 118 E18, 121, 124, 127, 130, 133, 136, 139, 142; *Ko*
174 A15, 179, 182, 185, 188, 191, 194, 199, 202, 207,
210, 213, 216.

155. White has paid too dearly for the life of his position on line 8. White has given away 25—30 points around P2 and just as many around C11.

171. The outcome of the game depends on this *Ko*.

217. White gives up the game.

[*Consecutive plays listed by the Editors*]

Black	White		
1. R16	2. P17	45. G4	46. B4
3. E17	4. D5	47. C4	48. B3
5. C16	6. P4	49. B5	50. A2
7. L17	8. C11	51. B1	52. C1
9. C3	10. E3	53. C7	54. E8
11. C5	12. C6	55. D9	56. G6
13. B6	14. D6	57. F2	58. A4
15. D4	16. E4	59. J3	60. N18
17. B7	18. L3	61. M16	62. N17
19. Q17	20. P16	63. L15	64. N14
21. Q14	22. M15	65. F10	66. G8
23. K16	24. R5	67. J5	68. K13
25. L14	26. N13	69. L13	70. J11
27. Q12	28. F16	71. F12	72. H13
29. E16	30. F14	73. E15	74. G11
31. D12	32. F17	75. M11	76. O11
33. L12	34. H16	77. L9	78. K8
35. O14	36. M17	79. L5	80. L8
37. M18	38. O15	81. M9	82. K4
39. E5	40. C2	83. J4	84. D11
41. B2	42. E7	85. E11	86. D10
43. F5	44. D2	87. E9	88. C12
		89. D13	90. C9

91. D8	92. K5	155. N1	156. C18
93. K6	94. J6	157. R10	158. C15
95. L6	96. L4	159. C14	160. B14
97. J7	98. H6	161. B15	162. C13
99. H9	100. H8	163. D15*	164. B12
101. J9	102. J8	165. B10	166. A13*
103. K9	104. K2	167. B9	168. A15
105. J2	106. N7	169. A16	170. B17
107. E2	108. D3	171. A14*	172. A1*
109. H2	110. E18	173. F4	174. A15 Ko
111. D18	112. G18	175. B16	176. E14
113. E19	114. F19	177. D14	178. D17*
115. F18*	116. G3	179. A14 Ko	180. H5
117. F3	118. E18 Ko	181. J1	182. A15 Ko
119. N3	120. N4	183. C17	184. B18
121. F18 Ko	122. E10	185. A14 Ko	186. Q16
123. G9	124. E18 Ko	187. R17	188. A15 Ko
125. O4	126. O5	189. A11	190. A12
127. F18 Ko	128. F11	191. A14 Ko	192. S15
129. E12	130. E18 Ko	193. S16	194. A15 Ko
131. O3	132. M5	195. P18	196. O18
133. F18 Ko	134. F8	197. Q18	198. N16
135. F9	136. E18 Ko	199. A14 Ko	200. H4
137. M8	138. M7	201. H3	202. A15 Ko
139. F18 Ko	140. R15	203. K18	204. P14
141. Q15	142. E18 Ko	205. Q13	206. P13
143. B13	144. D19*	207. A14 Ko	208. O2
145. Q2	146. R3	209. R1	210. A15 Ko
147. M2	148. L2	211. G12	212. H12
149. R2	150. S2	213. A14 Ko	214. P1
151. Q3	152. R4	215. P3	216. A15 Ko
153. M3	154. M4	217. P5	

Game VIII: White: Katsuda Eisuke

Black: Yasui Shintetsu   PLATE 25

(Played on the 16th of August, 1835)

This game is especially recommended to the attention of beginners because of the exceptional simplicity of the problems.

24. It would be much better to make use of C3 or D5. But both players dodge the contest.

37. Since White must develop E3 into a position in order to prevent Black's access to the large area at the lower margin, 37 L4 seems misplaced. With 37, Black gives up Upperhand, and White uses this with 38 to 42 in order to catch up with Black again.

54. The thought behind this play is not easily comprehended. If White had played at G18, his line H17—M14 would not have been broken.

72—80. White establishes the connection without losing Upperhand. Very elegant indeed.

96. Like move 54.

129. L5 is better than K4 by several points, but Black thereby loses Upperhand twice, which White utilizes through 138 and 152. With 129 K4 Black probably would have won.

207. Black sacrifices four points in order to free himself from *Ko* because White would prolong it.

[91]

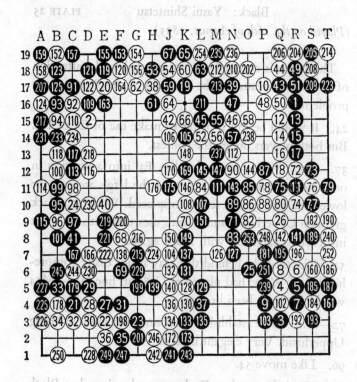

Plate 25

81 S11 Connects; *Ko* 162 B19, 165, 168, 171, 174, 177,
180, 183, 188, 191, 194, 197, 200, 203.

[Consecutive plays listed by the Editors]

Black	White
1. R16	2. D15
3. Q3	4. Q5
5. R5	6. R6
7. R4	8. Q6
9. P4	10. P17
11. R11	12. Q15
13. R15	14. Q14
15. R14	16. Q13
17. R13	18. Q12
19. K17	20. E17
21. C4	22. E3
23. G3	24. C10
25. O6	26. Q9
27. E4	28. D4
29. D5	30. D3
31. F4	32. C3
33. B5	34. B3
35. F2	36. E2
37. L4	38. H17
39. N17	40. E10
41. C8	42. J15
43. Q17	44. Q18
45. L15	46. N15
47. N16	48. P16
49. R18	50. Q16
51. R17	52. L14
53. H18	54. J18
55. M15	56. M14
57. N14	58. O15
59. J17	60. K18

Black	White
61. H16	62. G17
63. L18	64. J16
65. K19	66. K15
67. J19*	68. F8
69. F6	70. K9
71. N9	72. R12
73. S12	74. R10
75. Q11	76. S11
77. S10	78. P11
79. T11*	80. Q10
81. S11	82. O9
Connects	
83. N8	84. L11
85. O11	86. O10
87. P12	88. P10
89. N10	90. N12
91. C17	92. C16
93. B16	94. B15
95. B10	96. B9
97. C9	98. C11
99. B11	100. B12
101. B8	102. Q4
103. P3	104. J7
105. K14	106. J14
107. L10	108. K10
109. D16	110. C15
111. M11	112. N13
113. C12	114. A11
115. A9*	116. D12
117. C13	118. B13
119. E18	120. F18

121. D18	122. D17	185. S5	186. T6
123. B18	124. A16	187. T5	188. B19 *Ko*
125. B17	126. M7	189. S8	190. T9
127. N7	128. K5	191. A19 *Ko*	192. R3
129. L5	130. K4	193. S3*	194. B19 *Ko*
131. K6	132. J6	195. Q7	196. R7
133. K3	134. J3	197. A19 *Ko*	198. F3
135. L3	136. J4	199. G5	200. B19 *Ko*
137. K7	138. F7	201. G2	202. O18
139. H5	140. J5	203. A19 *Ko*	204. R19
141. R8	142. Q8	205. S19	206. Q19
143. N11	144. O12	207. A17*	208. S18
145. L12	146. K11	209. S17	210. N18
147. M12	148. K13*	211. L16	212. M18
149. K8	150. J8	213. M17	214. T19*
151. L9	152. B19	215. G7	216. G8
153. F19	154. G19	217. A15*	218. D13
155. E19	156. G18	219. E9	220. F9
157. C19	158. A18	221. E8	222. E7
159. A19*	160. S6	223. T17	224. H7
161. T4	162. B19 *Ko*	225. A4	226. A3
163. E16	164. F17	227. A5	228. D1
165. A19 *Ko*	166. D7	229. G6	230. D6
167. C7	168. B19 *Ko*	231. A14	232. D10
169. K12	170. J12	233. B14	234. C14*
171. A19 *Ko*	172. J2	235. M19	236. N19
173. K2	174. B19 *Ko*	237. M13	238. O14*
175. J11	176. H11	239. P5	240. T8
177. A19 *Ko*	178. B4	241. J1	242. H1
179. C5	180. B19 *Ko*	243. K1	244. C6
181. P7	182. S9	245. B6	246. H2
183. A19 *Ko*	184. S4	247. F1	248. P8

Game IX: White: Yasui Shintetsu
Black: Katsuda Eisuke   PLATE 26
(Played on the 12th of October, 1835)

19. White profits little by installing himself at R9—R12 and leaving Q3 as well as N17—P17 weak.

22. If White had applied 22 to an attack upon Black R5, then Black would perhaps have extended himself upon line C and then it would have become very difficult for White to penetrate by G3 or H3 into the Black position. Accordingly, Black secures R5. An attack upon C6 through C8 before securing R5 would be premature.

32 and 36. Make a penetration into the considerable territory at left difficult. But Black would do well to try first of all a feint by C13, then by C9. The attack at N16—N17 can still take place later.

52 and 56. If these moves had been properly applied to the threatened position, they would have saved it. Play 56 was especially pointless.

72. After White has finally lost the ten stones, he turns to the winning of the six Black stones. The question now is whether Black would do better to save these stones,

249. B1   250. O1   253. O8   254. L19*
251. P6   252. T7

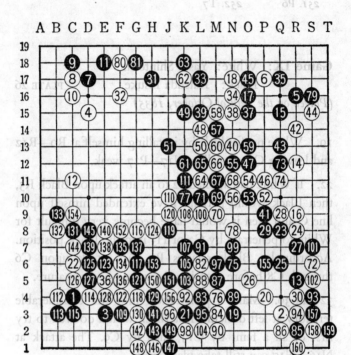

Plate 26

52 and 56. If these moves had been properly applied to
the threatened position, it would have saved it. Play
56 was especially pointless.

72. After White has finally lost the ten stones, he turns
to the winning of the six Black stones. The question now
is whether Black would do better to save these stones,

thereby certainly losing the territory at the lower edge of the board to White, or indeed give them up, and with their help first build K3—N3 further in order then to shift over to an energetic attack upon the White position on line C. This attack, which might well have been introduced earlier, still has a good deal in its favor since meanwhile the Black stones are advanced as far as K10 and a connection could easily be established with these.

79. Is obviously played in order to envelop the White position around S12, for Black's own position is already adequately protected. But Black loses in this every opportunity to save his six stones because he overlooked a play, but nevertheless he pushes forward an attempt at rescue. But even the stones that were directed towards effecting the rescue are enclosed, and Black surrenders.

[*Consecutive plays listed by the Editors*]

Black	White		
1. C4	2. Q3	21. K3	22. C6
3. E3	4. D15	23. Q8	24. R8
5. R16	6. P17	25. Q6	26. O5
7. D17	8. C17	27. R7	28. Q9
9. C18	10. C16	29. P8	30. R4
11. E18	12. C11	31. H17	32. F16
13. R5	14. R12	33. L17	34. N16
15. Q15	16. R9	35. Q17	36. E5
17. O16	18. N17	37. O15	38. N15
19. N3	20. P4	39. L15	40. N13
		41. P9	42. R14

43. Q13	44. S15	103. K5	104. L2*
45. O17	46. P11	105. K6	106. L4
47. O12	48. L14	107. K7	108. K9
49. K15	50. L13	109. F3	110. J10
51. J13	52. P10	111. K11*	112. B4
53. O10	54. O11	113. B3	114. D4
55. N12	56. N10	115. C3	116. G8
57. M14	58. M15	117. G6	118. G4
59. O13	60. M13	119. J8	120. J9
61. K12	62. K17	121. G5	122. F4
63. K18	64. L11	123. E6	124. H8
65. L12	66. M12	125. D6	126. C5
67. M11	68. N11	127. D5	128. E4
69. M10	70. M9	129. H4	130. G3
71. L10	72. S6	131. C8	132. B8
73. Q12	74. Q11	133. B9	134. F6
75. N6	76. M4	135. F7	136. F5
77. K10	78. N8	137. G7	138. E7
79. S16	80. F18	139. D7	140. E8
81. G18	82. L6	141. H3	142. G2
83. L4	84. M3	143. H2	144. C7
85. R2	86. Q2	145. D8	146. H1
87. M5	88. L5	147. J1	148. G1
89. N4	90. M2	149. J2	150. H5
91. L7	92. K4	151. J5	152. F8
93. S4	94. R3	153. H6*	154. C9
95. L3	96. J3	155. P6	156. J4
97. M6	98. K2	157. S3	158. S2
99. N7	100. L9	159. T2	160. R1*
101. S7	102. S5		

Game X: White: Sanchi

Black: Matsujiro PLATE 27

(Played on the 25th of November, 1840)

36—42. Show why White 30 and 32 were played. Further along Black 89 will follow from this.

49. Black does not wish to see White 30 repeated.

56. Both players have taken considerable territory and one is eager to see how they will manage to keep it. Black has the advantage because of the fact that White neglected D6 and E5 and played in a stereotyped way.

66. This is good. Because of it White is quite sure about Q17.

85. White cannot answer by P10; for, then Black would break out with K10 at left and make connection towards E8 or J4. And so White must play somewhere between N7 and G10 to prevent this connection; M7, for example—

B	W
—	M7
M5	H9
G8	P10 or K12

If Black tries to escape from K12 with P10, the way can still be cut off. Therefore K12 is better than P10 because Black then can no longer build two eyes.

86. G8 has been pushed forward too much, and Black 87 G10 destroys White 86 effectively.

[99]

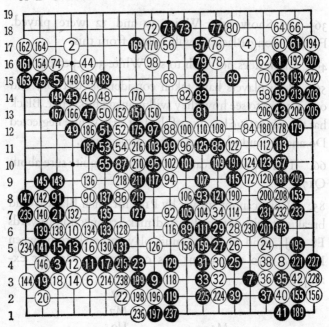

Plate 27

157 R3*; *Ko* 160 R2, 165, 168, 171, 174, 177, 182, 185, 188; *Ko* 212 T15; *Ko* 217 R3, 220, 222 R3 Connects; *Ko* 223 T16, 226 S17 Connects; 229 T15 Connects.

89. One now sees how good M7 would have been, since Black of his own accord makes the counter move.

111. White's loss will be some ten points, if he cannot take the five Black stones around M10. White plays 112—124 are directed to doing that. But Black secures two eyes because he has hindered White through 117 from occupying L9. After Black 125, White finds himself still some seven points behind, which he must now seek to attain by a minor skirmish.

126—146. With these plays White gains A2 and B3 as eyes and forces Black to fill up some of his eyes and, too, White gains Upperhand. The prior difference, however, is adjusted only by half.

155. White must accept *Ko*.

197. Black cannot go to H2 because it would entail:

B	W
—	G3
G4	H3
J4	H1*

White has lost by 4 points.

One might suppose that the seven White stones upon line K are not altogether lost, but might become *Seki*. Literally, *Seki* means *to possess* or *to occupy*. If two opposing chains that have no closed eyes are so situated with respect to each other that only two free places remain, then *Seki* arises, that is, the opponent's stones cannot be

89. One now sees how good M7 would have been, since Black of his own accord makes the counter move.

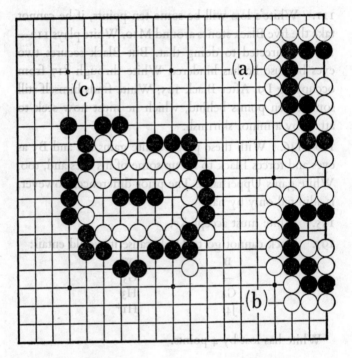

Plate 28

taken, because the one who first occupies one of the free points can instantly be taken by the other.

Seki would now take place in the middle of the field thus:

B	W
—	H5
J4	K5
L4	K8
L9	G7
F9	H6
J7	Seki

Black will, however, place not F9, but, rather, H6.

H6	F9
D9 or D8	E7*
F7	

and White is dead, whereby the Black stones standing in *Seki* become free; in contrast the White stones die as the others did.

Plate 28 shows some cases of *Seki*, which are immediately clear on inspection. The simplest example of *Seki* is shown in diagram (a). Diagram (b) is no longer *Seki* since White by means of his possession of the free point upon T kills the Black stones. Among skilled players *Seki* seldom or never occurs.

[Consecutive plays listed by the Editors]

Black	White		
1. R16	2. D17	5. C15	6. E3
3. C4	4. P17	7. P3	8. R4
		9. J3	10. D6

11. E4	12. D4	75. B15	76. N17
13. D5	14. D3	77. N18	78. N16
15. C5	16. E5	79. M16	80. O18
17. F4	18. C3	81. M13	82. L14
19. B3	20. B2	83. M14	84. P12
21. C7	22. G2	85. N11	86. G8
23. H4	24. Q5	87. G10	88. K12
25. O4	26. O5	89. L6	90. E8
27. N5	28. O6	91. C8	92. K7
29. N6	30. N4	93. M8	94. K9
31. M4	32. N3	95. J10	96. L11
33. M3	34. N7	97. J12	98. J16
35. R3	36. Q3	99. K11	100. L12
37. Q2	38. Q4	101. L10	102. K10
39. O2	40. R2	103. J11	104. M7
41. R1	42. S3*	105. L7	106. L8
43. R13	44. E16	107. M9	108. N12
45. D14	46. E14	109. N10	110. M12
47. E13	48. F14	111. M6	112. Q11
49. D12	50. F13	113. R11	114. O7
51. F12	52. G12	115. O9	116. K6
53. F11	54. G11	117. J9	118. K3
55. F10	56. K17	119. K2	120. Q9
57. M17	58. Q14	121. N8	122. O11
59. R14	60. R17	123. Q10	124. P10
61. S17	62. Q16	125. M11	126. J5
63. R15	64. R18	127. H7	128. G6
65. M15	66. S18	129. K4	130. F5
67. R10	68. K15	131. G5	132. D7
69. O15	70. Q15	133. F6	134. E6
71. K18	72. J18	135. F7	136. E9
73. L18	74. C16	137. F8	138. C6

139. B6	*140.* B7	*193.* S15	*194.* T17*
141. B5	*142.* B8	*195.* S5	*196.* J2
143. C9	*144.* A3	*197.* J1	*198.* H2
145. B9	*146.* B4*	*199.* H3	*200.* Q8
147. A8	*148.* D15	*201.* Q6	*202.* T15
149. C14	*150.* J13	*203.* T14	*204.* S13
151. H13	*152.* G13	*205.* T13	*206.* Q13
153. S8	*154.* B16	*207.* T16*	*208.* R8
155. S2	*156.* T2	*209.* S9	*210.* H10
157. R3*	*158.* L5	*211.* H9	*212.* T15 *Ko*
159. M5	*160.* R2 *Ko*	*213.* S14*	*214.* F3
161. A16	*162.* A17	*215.* G4	*216.* H11
163. A15	*164.* B17	*217.* R3 *Ko*	*218.* G9
165. R3 *Ko*	*166.* D13	*219.* H8	*220.* R2 *Ko*
167. C13*	*168.* R2 *Ko*	*221.* S4	*222.* R3
169. H17	*170.* J17		Connects
171. R3 *Ko*	*172.* P9	*223.* T16 *Ko*	*224.* N2
173. R6	*174.* R2 *Ko*	*225.* M2	*226.* S17
175. H12	*176.* H14		Connects
177. R3 *Ko*	*178.* R12	*227.* T4	*228.* T3
179. S12	*180.* Q12	*229.* T15	*230.* P6
181. R9	*182.* R2 *Ko*	*231.* Q7	*232.* R7
183. F15	*184.* E15	*233.* S7	*234.* A5
185. R3 *Ko*	*186.* E12	*235.* A7*	*236.* H1
187. E11*	*188.* R2 *Ko*	*237.* K1	*238.* G3
189. S1	*190.* O8		
191. O10	*192.* S16		

231. Q7 with "Connects" note appears under column.

Game XI: White: Matsujiro
Black: Sanchi   PLATE 29
(Played on the 29th of June, 1841)

In this game the action is very lively. Major positions arise over and over up until the end.

12—25. The same opening as 10—23 of the prior game. Now, however, D6 and E5 are strengthened through White 26. From this follows a long drawn out struggle.

62. Gives White an advantage, because Black must now support G9 which is totally unsupported.

88 and 92. The flight of the Black stones upon line 10 is diverted toward line J. To drive them still farther with H11 and K12 and then to create a considerable territory with J17 will not work out because Black could quite well destroy White with D15 and keep the territory about R15 himself.

149. The White position in the middle can now only live by means of *Ko*.

151. Black lives at the lower edge.

160. Black at the lower edge right has only one eye. Now it depends upon whether Black or White in the center will be taken first.

171. Black disregards the *Ko* threat at 170, and rightly, because through 171 Black is safe around H12 and Black's victory is thereby quite likely.

245. White throws in the sponge. He, of course, has won the thirteen Black stones along the left margin, since they can be completely surrounded with only six plays, whereas the White position in the middle requires eight plays to be surrounded, but nineteen White stones are lost on the upper center and margin. Also, of the eleven White stones around Q10 the five stones on lines P and O would die, and although they could still be developed into a safe position even then the loss of the game would be inevitable.

[*Consecutive plays listed by the Editors*]

Black	White		
1. C4	2. Q3	33. E7	34. G6
3. R16	4. E16	35. E8	36. J5
5. P16	6. E3	37. H2	38. G3
7. R5	8. R9	39. G4	40. L3
9. R11	10. P4	41. H6	42. G7
11. J3	12. D6	43. J6	44. H8
13. E4	14. D4	45. K5	46. F10
15. D5	16. D3	47. B9	48. B10
17. C5	18. E5	49. A9	50. D1
19. F4	20. C3	51. C16	52. C17
21. B3	22. B2	53. B17	54. D17
23. C7	24. G2	55. B15	56. L17
25. H4	26. E6	57. M4	58. M3
27. B4	28. C9	59. G9	60. F9
29. A2	30. B1	61. F8	62. G8
31. C8	32. D9	63. G10	64. G11
		65. H10	66. K8

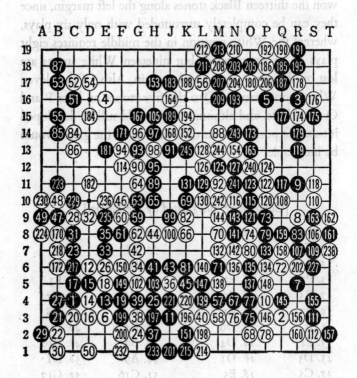

Plate 29

Ko 101 G13, 104, 113, 166, 169; *Ko* 216 M18, 219, 222, 225; *Ko* 226 S8; *Ko* 228 M18, 231, 234, 237, 239 M18 Connects.

67. N4	68. O2	131. K11	132. M7
69. K10	70. M8	133. P7	134. P6
71. M6	72. Q6	135. O6	136. N6
73. P9	74. O8	137. O5	138. M5
75. O3	76. N3	139. L4	140. L6*
77. O4	78. P2	141. N8	142. N7
79. P8	80. O7	143. N9	144. M9
81. K6	82. K9	145. Q4	146. P3
83. R8	84. C14	147. L5	148. P5
85. B14	86. C13	149. F5	150. F6
87. B18	88. M14	151. K2	152. K14
89. H11	90. G12	153. H17	154. N13
91. J13	92. M11	155. S4	156. R3
93. G13	94. F13	157. T2	158. Q7
95. H12	96. G14	159. Q8	160. R2
97. H14	98. H13*	161. T8	162. T9
99. J9	100. J8	163. S9*	164. J16
101. G13 Ko	102. G5	165. O13	166. H13 Ko
103. H5	104. H13Ko	167. G15	168. J14
105. H15	106. S8	169. G13 Ko	170. B8
107. R7	108. Q10	171. F14*	172. B6
109. S7	110. S10	173. O14	174. R15
111. S3	112. S2	175. S15	176. S16
113. G13 Ko	114. F12	177. Q15	178. R17
115. O10	116. N10	179. R14*	180. O17
117. Q11	118. S11	181. E13	182. D11
119. R13	120. P10	183. J17	184. D15
121. O9	122. P11	185. Q18	186. P18
123. O11	124. P12	187. Q17	188. K17
125. M12	126. L12	189. J15	190. Q19
127. N12	128. L13	191. R19	192. K19
129. L11	130. L10	193. N16	194. K15

195. R18	*196.* K3	*223.* B11	*224.* A8
197. H3	*198.* L2	*225.* M19 *Ko*	*226.* S8 *Ko*
199. F3	*200.* F2	*227.* S6	*228.* M18 *Ko*
201. J1	*202.* R6	*229.* C10	*230.* A10*
203. N18	*204.* N17	*231.* M19 *Ko*	*232.* F1
205. O18	*206.* P17	*233.* H1	*234.* M18 *Ko*
207. M17	*208.* M18	*235.* E9	*236.* E10
209. M16	*210.* N19	*237.* M19 *Ko*	*238.* T7*
211. L18	*212.* L19	*239.* M18	*240.* O12
213. M19*	*214.* L1	Connects	
215. K1	*216.* M18 *Ko*	*241.* N11	*242.* M10
217. C6	*218.* B7	*243.* N14	*244.* M13
219. M19 *Ko*	*220.* K4	*245.* K13	
221. J4*	*222.* M18 *Ko*		

Game XII: White: Matsujiro

Black: Sanchi

PLATE 30

(Played on the 2nd of December, 1842)

26. This play was to be expected, although White does not attain a favorable situation by means of it.

74. The play from 26 on is choice. Black maintains the ascendancy.

88. The retreat of Black 65 to 5 or 87 is upset through this play. Consequently, Black at once seeks to win eyes for his position by means of 89 and give up Upperhand. Hence, White obtains the position around R16.

90—102. Black suffers a severe loss through these plays, but he has also gained through them the strong alignment upon line Q, which he uses from 103 on to launch a forceful and rewarding attack against J17—N17.

133. This shows why Black did not retort to White 128. With 129 Black gives away the position around B4, of which White seizes possession by means of 130 and 132, and Black protects himself at K17 instead.

181. This and the next play, isolating the White stones around N17, initiate Black's victory. With Black 227 N19 the death of these White stones is decided and therewith the victory. One could already foresee the outcome at Black 197 D16.

Black has won by 10 points.

[Consecutive plays listed by the Editors]

Black	White		
1. C4	2. Q3	29. G2	30. B3
3. R16	4. E16	31. B4	32. F2
5. P16	6. E3	33. J3	34. H6
7. R5	8. R8	35. F6	36. K4
9. Q8	10. R9	37. K3	38. L4
11. C16	12. C17	39. J5	40. E9
13. B17	14. D17	41. J6	42. H7
15. B15	16. J17	43. F8	44. H9
17. G3	18. N3	45. F9	46. K7
19. E4	20. D3	47. L5	48. E11
21. D4	22. F3	49. G10	50. F12
23. F4	24. C3	51. M5	52. O5
25. D13	26. G4	53. M2	54. C8
27. H4	28. G5	55. G12	56. G13
		57. H12	58. D6

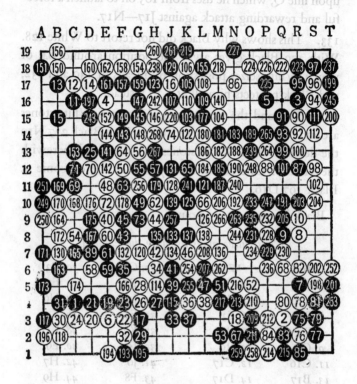

Plate 30

Ko 113 K17, 116, 119, 124, 127, 221 K16 Connects; 246
S15 Connects; 269 P7*; 270 P8*; 271 P9; 272 P7 Connects.

59. E6	60. E8	123. H17	124. K16 Ko
61. E7	62. H10	125. K10	126. L9
63. F11	64. F13	127. K17 Ko	128. J11
65. K12	66. L10	129. J18*	130. B7
67. N2	68. Q6	131. J12	132. F7
69. C11	70. D12	133. J8	134. J7
71. C12	72. E10	135. H8	136. M7
73. G9	74. J14	137. K8	138. L8
75. R3	76. R2	139. J10	140. M16
77. S2	78. R4	141. E13	142. E12
79. S3	80. Q4	143. F14	144. E14
81. S4	82. R6	145. G15	146. H15
83. Q2	84. P2	147. G16	148. G14
85. R1*	86. N17	149. F15	150. B18
87. R12	88. P12	151. A18	152. E15
89. D7	90. R15	153. C13	154. G18
91. Q15	92. R14	155. L18	156. B19
93. Q14	94. S16	157. F17	158. F18
95. R17	96. S17	159. G17	160. D18
97. S18	98. S12	161. E17	162. E18
99. Q13	100. R13	163. B6	164. B9
101. Q12	102. S11	165. C7	166. F5
103. K15	104. M15	167. D8	168. C10
105. K17	106. K18	169. B11	170. B10
107. J16	108. L17	171. A7	172. B8
109. L16	110. K16*	173. A5	174. C5
111. S15	112. S14	175. D9	176. D10
113. K17 Ko	114. H5	177. L15	178. F10
115. J4	116. K16 Ko	179. H11	180. L14
117. A3	118. B2	181. M14	182. M13
119. K17 Ko	120. G7	183. N14	184. L12
121. L11	122. K14	185. M12	186. L13

187. M11	188. N13	231. O8	232. P9
189. O14	190. N12	233. O10	234. O7
191. Q10	192. N10	235. O9	236. P6*
193. F1	194. E1	237. T18	238. H18
195. G1	196. A2	239. O13	240. N11
197. D16	198. S5	241. K11*	242. H16
199. T17	200. T15*	243. D15	244. N8
201. T5	202. S6	245. T16	246. S15
203. R10	204. S10		Connects
205. Q9	206. M10	247. P10	248. O12
207. L6	208. L7	249. A10	250. A9
209. O3	210. O4	251. A11	252. T6
211. O2	212. P3	253. T4	254. K6
213. N4	214. P1	255. K5	256. G11*
215. Q1	216. N5	257. J9*	258. O1
217. M4	218. M18	259. N1	260. H19
219. K19*	220. J15	261. J19	262. M6
221. K16	222. Q18	263. N9	264. P13
Connects		265. P14	266. M9
223. R18	224. O18	267. H13	268. H14
225. P17	226. P18	269. P7*	270. P8*
227. N19	228. P8	271. P9	272. P7
229. P7	230. Q7		Connects

V
Problems

(*From the work* GOKYO SHUMYO)

THE EXAMPLES from Chapter IV should suffice to give a good overall view of the game of *Go*. All of the examples chosen there may be regarded as of certified standard form, inasmuch as none of the players is of a rank less than the Fifth. Even such a basic survey of models, however, is not sufficient in order to understand *Go* thoroughly. It is also necessary to be acquainted with the openings which have accumulated in Japan in order to come to terms with the game fully.

First, there is the so-called *Joseki,* that is, literally, the "steady stones" or, as we would say, the theory of openings. Just as in chess, the great masters have attentively studied the openings in *Go* because the whole game follows from these. In recent times, especially, decided advances have been made in the sorts of openings. More subtle *Joseki* have been distinguished from one another and identified, as, for example, in the period Tempo (1830–1844 A.D.).

Then, too, there are now quite abundant collections of Problems that can stand about side by side with our chess exercises. Certain positions that re-occur typically or which have proven themselves especially interesting are distinguished and the exercise consists in trying to keep them alive, to kill them, to turn them to account by *Ko*, etc. The solutions, which are for the most part rather difficult to find, are usually supplied in an appendix. Actually, the solution of such problems is far from being as pointless an undertaking as the solutions of chess problems usually turn out to be. With a *Go* exercise, one can as a rule with some reflection establish a predictable situation because the number of possibilities is relatively limited. But the task is not merely to solve the problems; one must retain the solutions in mind severally and jointly, or at least those that turn up over and over. Thus armed with foresight one need never stumble blindly into losing a position and with it the game. When one knows in advance how to evaluate the implications of a position and when danger is really lurking there, one need not be put off one's play by the attack of an opponent who is confident that he has finished off the situation, and one can so gain Upperhand. Thus forearmed, a player can develop a dashing and aggressive style of play, which is only apparently rash, however, because it is actually based on an exact comprehension of the game.

Then there are collections of end plays, making available the most advantageous lines of play and the number of points each is worth. It is strictly necessary to learn these; for, in games with only a slight difference of points, and these are the most frequent in occurrence, that player will win who knows the immediately available end plays better, and, accordingly, in the sequence in which he plays them, makes the lesser number of errors.

This chapter will deal with Problems, to be followed by a chapter on End Plays, and finally by a chapter on Openings since Master Murase is presently still writing his "Theory of Openings" and will publish his work in the near future at which time I will have the benefit of his thoughts.

Problems fall into the following classifications:

1. *To make positions alive, although they reasonably look hopeless.*

2. *To kill positions.*

3. *To bring positions to* Ko. What will eventuate from these positions does not depend on them as such but upon the greater number of risky situations held by one player rather than another.

4. *To hem in chains reciprocally.* Chains without eyes are so intermixed with each other that one of them must die, whereby the other is then converted into a secure position with eyes.

5. *To rescue certain weak stones.* If certain stones (which are in the vicinity of the margin but without a stable base) are separated *by* an enemy formation (which does not touch on the margin but only approaches it) *from* a friendly position that has been formed by an extraneous chain, then the task is to slip by or through the enemy

formation and to connect the unstable stones to the nearby extraneous chain that is stable.

6. *The Robber's Play* (Oi-otoshi). An opponent apparently has a chain totally in his power. By the insertion of new stones which the opponent is forced to take, one compels him to fill his territory so full that finally he has to sacrifice a part of his chain being isolated by his enemy in order to avoid a greater loss. This sort of play is the superlative of finesse. It derives its special name from the fact that the opponent feels himself entirely safe and, not expecting an attack in the least, is overwhelmed when it comes, as if he had been ambushed by a robber.

7. *To dismember a loose enemy chain.* An eyeless chain is surrounded and isolated by means of an enemy chain which still has gaps. These gaps should then be penetrated and one must cut off from the hostile chain a strip which in turn is surrounded and killed.

Examples of each type of problem are given below in summary form. The numbers from 1 to 52 refer to 52 different displays each on a separate plate.* Following each number is a listing of positions for White stones and a listing of positions for Black stones. When the stones are placed on the points given, they will group themselves naturally into not more than four different problems diagrammed in different sections of the plate and designated as follows: (c)   (a)

(d)   (b)

*[See Plates 31–82, supplied by the Editors.]

After the listings of White and Black stones, the color that plays first for each problem is given in abbreviated form; thus, "a,d—W b,c—B," means that White plays first in sections (a) and (d) of the plate, and Black plays first in sections (b) and (c) of the plate.

Solutions are given immediately following the listing of all of the problems.

1. To make positions alive.

1. W A14, B3, 11, 13, C3, 13, 14, 15, 17, D2, 17, 18, E2, 16, F17, O3, Q3, 4, 18, R3, 5, 18, S5, 16, 17, 18.

   B A13, B4, 14, 15, 17, 18, C4, 16, 18, D3, E3, F2, G3, O17, P18, Q17, R2, 4, 15, 17, S3, 4, 15.

   a,d—W   b,c—B   [Plate 31]

2. W B5, 12, 13, 15, 16, C4, 13, 15, D5, 13, 14, E2, 3, 4, G2, M16, 17, N16, O1, 15, 17, P2, 14, 17, Q2, 3, 18, R3, 14, S3, 4, 15.

   B A16, B3, 4, 11, 17, C10, 12, 16, D2, 3, 12, 15, 16, E1, 13, 14, N2, 17, O2, 16, P1, 3, 4, 16, Q4, 16, R4, 6, 16, S5, 16, 18, T4.

   a,d—B   b,c—W   [Plate 32]

3. W A4, B5, 6, 15, 16, C4, 17, 18, D5, 18, E2, 3, 4, L18, M16, 17, N14, 18, O13, 19, P18, Q3, 12, 13, 17, 18, R2, 3, 12, 14, 18, S3, 14, 17, 19.

   B A5, 15, B3, 4, 14, C3, 14, 15, 16, D2, 3, 17, E17, 18, N17, O15, 17, 18, P2, 3, 5, 14, 17, Q2, 4, 14, 15, 16, R5, 7, 13, 16, 17, S13, 18.

   a,d—B   b,c—W   [Plate 33]

4. W A16, B2, 15, C3, 15, 16, D1, 3, 17, E2, 17, F18, G18, Q15, R3, 4, 5, 14, 15, 16, S2, 17.

[119]

B B4, 16, 17, C5, 17, D4, 18, E3, 4, 18, F1, 2, 19,
G3, O3, P3, 15, 17, Q4, 6, 13, 14, 16, R6, 11,
12, 17, 18, S6, T3.

$$a,b,d—W \qquad c—B \qquad [Plate \; 34]$$

5. **W** B4, C3, 4, 5, 13, 15, 16, 17, E4, 14, 15, 16, F2,
3, H2, M17, N18, O17, 19, P2, 3, 6, 15, 17, Q2,
4, R2, 4, 6, 7, 14, 16, S16.

B B3, 14, 15, C2, 12, 14, D3, 13, 17, E2, 12, 17,
F1, 15, 16, G13, O18, P18, Q3, 16, 17, R1, 3,
9, 17, S2, 4, 5, 17.

$$a,b,d—B \qquad c—W \qquad [Plate \; 35]$$

6. **W** B13, 14, 16, C7, 13, D3, 5, 6, 13, 14, 15, 18,
E2, 3, 7, 16, 17, F5, O2, 3, 4, 6, Q4, 17, R4, 6,
16, 17, S5, 18, T4.

B B15, C2, 4, 5, 6, 9, 10, 14, 15, 17, 18, D2, 16,
E8, F2, 8, G3, 5, 6, J3, N17, O17, P2, 3, 16,
Q16, R3, 15, S3, 4, 16, 17.

$$a,d—W \qquad b,c—B \qquad [Plate \; 36]$$

7. **W** A2, B3, 4, C5, D4, 6, E4, 17, 18, F3, 16, G2, 3,
16, H16, 17, N17, O3, 17, 18, P3, 16, Q2, 16,
R3, 15, S16, 18, T2.

B B1, 2, C3, 4, 16, D3, 15, 17, E3, 14, F2, G15,
J14, 16, 18, K17, L13, 15, N3, 4, O2, P2, 5, 17,
18, Q17, R4, 6, 17, S4, 17.

$$a,d—B \qquad b,c—W \qquad [Plate \; 37]$$

8. **W** B4, 13, 17, C2, 3, 4, 13, 14, 18, D3, E14, 17,
18, G15, J15, 17, 18, L2, 3, M3, N4, O4, P6,
Q15, R4, 5, 7, 13, 14, S2, 3, 11, 12, 15, 16.

B B2, 3, 5, 14, 15, 16, C5, 7, 16, D4, 16, E4, 16,
F3, 16, G17, 18, H3, M2, N2, 3, P3, 13, 15, 16,

Q4, 10, 16, R2, 3, 11, 12, 15, 16, S10, 17.
a,d—W   b,c—B   [Plate 38]

9. W   C5, 15, 16, 17, D3, 5, 7, 14, E4, 5, F4, 13, 14,
17, G3, 12, 17, H3, J2, 13, 14, K15, 16, 17, M17,
Q17.

   B   B5, 6, C3, 4, D4, 6, 16, E3, 6, F6, 16, G14, 16,
H5, 14, 17, J16, 17, K3, 5, 14, L3, P3.
a—B   b—W   [Plate 39]

10. W   B5, 6, C8, D2, 3, 8, 17, E8, 16, 17, F3, 6, 7, 16,
18, G16, H16, J17, K1, L2, M2, N3, 4, O3, P3,
4, 16, 17, 18, Q1, 2, 3, 15, R15, S15, T18.

   B   B4, C3, 5, 17, D5, 7, 15, 16, 18, E6, 14, 18, F17,
G14, H2, J1, 14, K2, 3, 5, 15, 17, 18, L15, 17,
M3, 4, N5, O2, 4, 5, P5, Q4, 16, 17, 18, R2, 3,
5, 16, S16.   a,d—B   b,c—W   [Plate 40]

11. W   B3, C3, 7, D3, 6, 13, 18, E3, 6, 13, 14, 15, 16,
17, 18, F4, 5, 6, G16, 17, 18, H18, L4, M4, N2,
3, O4, P4, Q2, 3, 4, R2, 4, 8, 12, 13, 14, S8, 12,
15, 16.

   B   C4, 6, 8, 12, 13, 18, D5, 7, 8, 14, 15, 16, 17,
19, E4, 5, 11, F3, 8, 12, G3, 4, 7, 14, H6, 15, 16,
17, J3, 18, K4, 17, L3, 5, 6, M2, N5, P5, 6, 11,
13, Q9, 11, 13, 15, 17, R1, 3, 5, 6, 16, S2, 3, 4,
9, 11, 17.   a,b,c,d—W   [Plate 41]

12. W   B8, 10, C5, 6, 7, 9, D2, 9, E3, 8, F5, 7, G3, J16,
17, K2, 16, 18, L2, 16, M1, 3, 14, 16, N3, 4,
15, O4, 15, P2, 4, 6, 15, 16, Q1, 2, 3, 16, R3, 6,
16, 17, 18, S1, 2.

   B   B9, C2, 3, 8, D4, 5, 6, 7, 8, G18, H15, 17, J2,
18, K3, 14, 17, L3, 14, 17, 18, M2, 13, 17, N2,

13, O1, 2, 3, 16, 17, P3,8, 13, Q4, 17, 18, R2, 4, 8, 13, 15, S3, 4, 6, 15, T2.

a,b—W c—B   [Plate 42]

13. W B2, 10, 18, 19, C2, 3, 8, 9, 10, 17, D5, 6, 7, 17, E3, 17, G17, 18, M17, N16, O3, 13, 15, 17, 18, P3, 18, Q3, 13, R2, 12, 14, 15, 17, 18, S2.

B A18, B3, 4, 7, 8, 9, 15, 17, C4, 7, 16, 18, D15, F16, G16, H16, 18, J17, K17, M3, N2, 4, O4, 16, P14, 16, 17, Q4, 14, 16, 18, 19, R3, 5, 7, 16, S3. a,d—B b,c—W   [Plate 43]

14. W B10, 17, C3, 4, 10, 15, 16, D3, 10, 12, 17, E1, 3, 13, 15, F2, K2, L3, 5, M2, N3, 6, O2, 3, P3, 6, 18, 19, Q17, R5, 6, 17, S4, 17.

B B5, 11, 15, 16, C5, 11, 13, 14, D2, 4, 5, F3, 4, G2, H3, M3, 4, N2, 4, O4, 17, 18, P4, 17, Q2, 4, 16, R3, 19, S3, 15, 16.

a,d—W b,c—B   [Plate 44]

2. To kill positions.

15. W B4, 15, 18, C3, 4, 16, 17, E1, 3, F2, 4, G2, O17, P5, 18, Q3, 14, 15, 16, 17, R2, 5, 13, S5, 6, 13, 14, 15.

B A3, B2, 3, 14, C2, 14, D2, 15, 16, 17, 18, E2, F1, O2, P3, 4, 6, Q2, 5, 18, R6, 7, 14, 15, 16, 17, 18, S8, 16, T15.

a,d—W b,c—B   [Plate 45]

16. W B4, 16, C4, 10, D3, 13, 15, 16, 17, E3, F2, G3, P17, 18, Q1, 15, 16, R2, 3, 5, 13, 15, S5.

B A3, B3, 14, C2, 12, 15, D2, 18, E2, 12, F14, 15, 17, G17, O2, Q2, 3, 4, 5, 6, 17, 18, R7, 16, S7, 16.

a,d—W b,c—B   [Plate 46]

17. W B5, 15, C5, 8, 15, 17, 18, D5, E2, 4, F2, 3, 4,

M16, O15, 16, 18, P18, Q2, 14, R2, 12, 15, 18, S3, 4, 5, 16.

B   B4, 14, C4, 12, 14, D2, 3, 15, 16, 17, E3, F17, L16, P2, 3, 16, 17, Q3, 16, 18, R4, 5, 7, S6, 17, 18.

　　　　　 a,d—W　 *b,c—B*　　 *[Plate 47]*

18.　W   B14, C3, 4, 6, 17, E3, 17, F2, 3, 17, G17, P17, 18, Q15, 17, R2, 4, 5, 13, 15, S2, 3.

B   B3, 13, C2, 13, 14, 15, D2, E2, 16, F15, H15, 16, 18, J17, Q2, 3, 4, 5, 6, 18, R3, 7, 16, 17, S16.

　　　　　 a,d—W　 *b,c—B*　　 *[Plate 48]*

19.　W   B4, C4, 6, 17, 18, D4, E3, 16, 17, F3, 15, G2, 16, H3, 16, 17, K16, N17, P2, 16, 17, 18, Q2, 15, R3, 13, 15, S14.

B   B3, 17, 18, C3, 16, D3, 14, 16, 17, E2, 13, 15, F2, G14, 15, 17, J14, 15, K17, L16, N3, O3, Q3, 4, 16, 17, 18, R5, 16, S15.

　　　　　 a,d—W　 *b,c—B*　　 *[Plate 49]*

20.　W   A4, 11, B3, 5, 11, 15, 16, 17, C4, 5, 10, 13, 14, D5, 12, E4, F4, G4, H3, O2, 16, 17, 18, P2, 14, 15, 18, Q3, 4, 6, R6, 13, 15, S3, 4, 15, T2.

B   A16, 17, B2, 9, 10, 18, C3, 8, 11, 15, 17, D3, 4, 9, 15, 17, E3, 12, 13, 17, F3, 10, M3, N2, O1, 3, 4, 6, P16, 17, Q7, 18, R7, 16, 17, S1, 2, 5, 6, 16.　　 *a,d—W*　 *b,c—B*　　 *[Plate 50]*

21.　W   B16, 17, C17, D18, 19, H3, K3, 4, M3, 17, N4, O2, 16, 17, P3, 4, 15, Q6, R5, 13, 15, S1, 4, 15, 16.

B   C12, 14, 16, D16, 17, E18, F17, P1, 2, 16, Q3, 16, 18, R2, 3, 16, S3, 17.

　　　　　 a,b—W　　 *c—B*　　 *[Plate 51]*

22.　W   A4, B3, 5, 19, C4, 5, 18, D5, E4, 5, 18, F3, 17,

[123]

18, G2, 3, H3, K17, 18, L16, M16, N16, O16,
P15, Q15, R2, 3, 4, 15, 17, S1, 17, T2.

B A2, B2, 13, C3, 14, 15, 19, D3, 4, 16, 18, E3,
17, 19, F2, 4, L17, 18, N17, O17, P6, 16, Q1,
2, 3, 4, 17, R1, 5, 18, S5.

a,d—W   b,c—B   [Plate 52]

23. W A3, 15, B1, 3, 7, 15, C6, 16, 17, 18, D5, E4,
F4, G2, 3, N17, O15, 16, 18, P15, Q2, 4, R4,
5, 13, 15, S2, 15, 16.

B B4, 14, C3, 4, 14, 15, D1, 3, 16, 17, 18, 19, E3,
F2, P2, 3, 4, 16, Q5, 6, 17, 18, R2, 6, 8, 16, S17.

a,d—W   b,c—B   [Plate 53]

3. To bring positions to Ko.

24. W B4, 16, 17, C4, 18, D4, E3, 4, F2, G4, O4, 5, 16
P2, 3, 6, 17, 18, Q16, R2, 6, 7, 14, 16, S3, 5,
15.

B C2, 3, 13, 15, 16, 17, D3, 18, E2, 17, L3, N3, 4,
O3, P4, Q4, 17, 18, R4, 9, 17, S4, 7, 16, T4.

a,b,d—B   c—W   [Plate 54]

25. W B4, C4, 15, 16, 17, D3, 18, E3, F2, 3, P17, 18,
Q3, 17, R3, 15, 16, S4, 15.

B B3, 14, C1, 3, 12, 14, D2, 15, 16, 17, E2, 18,
F17, O3, P3, Q4, 18, R4, 6, 17, 19, S5, 16, 17.

a,b,c,d—W   [Plate 55]

26. W B5, 15, 16, C4, 5, 17, 18, D19, E4, F4, H2, 4,
5, J3, N17, O18, P2, 16, 17, Q2, 16, R3, 4, 16,
S2, 16.

B B3, 4, 14, 18, C14, 15, D3, 16, 18, E3, 18, F3,
16, G3, M3, O3, P3, 18, Q5, 17, R5, 17, S3,
4, 17, T2.   a—B   b,c,d—W   [Plate 56]

27. W B12, C5, 8, 12, 13, 14, 18, D9, 10, 15, 16, 17,
19, E18, P18, Q17, R4, 5, 6, 7, 17, S17.

B A12, B11, 13, 14, 18, C10, 15, 16, 17, O17, 18,
P4, 16, Q3, 5, 7, 8, 16, R3, 9, 10, 16, S16, 18.
a,b,c—W [Plate 57]

28. W A2, B3, 4, C5, 15, 16, 17, D4, 5, 16, F4, G2, 3,
N17, O18, P16, 17, Q15, R2, 4, 15, S3, 16.

B B2, C3, 4, 14, D3, 14, 15, 17, 18, E3, 16, F2,
17, O3, P4, 18, Q2, 4, 16, 17, R5, 6, S4, 17.
a,d—B   b,c—W [Plate 58]

29. W B2, 5, 18, C5, 17, D4, 16, E2, 3, 4, 16, F17, M2,
N3, 4, P15, 18, Q3, 4, 13, 17, R2, 4, 11, 13, 18,
S2, 12, T3.

B A2, 18, B4, 16, 17, C4, 14, D2, 3, E15, F15, G16,
17, 18, L2, 3, M5, N5, P5, 6, R3, 5, 14, 16, 17,
S3, 4, 5, 13, T4.
a,b,d—B   c—W [Plate 59]

30. W A18, B12, 19, C12, 17, 18, D2, 13, 14, 15, E3,
16, 17, F3, 5, G2, J3, K3, P15, 16, 18, Q15, 17,
R16, 17, S17.

B B13, 17, 18, C2, 3, 14, 15, 16, D3, 5, 16, F6,
G3, 5, K4, 5, L3, M2, 4, N17, O15, 17, 18, P14,
17, 19, Q14, R14, S15, 16.
a—W   b,c—B [Plate 60]

31. W B17, C5, 8, 16, D15, 16, 17, E2, 4, F1, 3, 4, G4,
K15, 17, L15, 17, M15, O2, 14, 15, 17, P2, Q14,
R3, 15, 17, S3, 4, 15, 17.

B B16, C14, 15, D3, 14, E3, 14, 15, 17, F2, 17,
G2, 3, H2, 3, 17, M16, 17, N2, 3, 16, O4, 16,
18, P3, 16, 17, Q4, 16, R4, 6, 16, S5, T5.
a,d—W   b,c—B [Plate 61]

32. W B4, 15, 18, C2, 3, 5, 6, 16, 18, D1, 16, 18, E1,
6, 17, F4, 5, G5, J3, 6, K3, 5, L3, P17, 18, 19,
Q2, 13, 15, 16, 19, R2, 3, 4, 6, 7, 14, S2, 4, 6,
13, T14.

B B14, C4, 11, 14, D2, 3, 4, 17, 19, E15, 16, 18,
F2, 3, 18, G4, 15, 16, H2, 4, J2, P2, 3, 7, Q1,
4, 5, 8, 18, R8, 16, 19, S7, 8, 18, T6, 16.

a—W   b,c,d—B   [Plate 62]

4. To hem in chains reciprocally.

33. W B2, 3, 4, 15, 16, C5, 15, 17, 18, D3, 4, 6, 17,
E18, F3, G2, 3, N17, O3, P2, 17, Q2, 17, R3,
17, S3, 5, 18.

B B5, 6, 17, C2, 3, 4, 7, 16, D2, 16, 18, E2, 16,
17, F2, 18, Q3, 4, 18, R2, 6, 14, 16, 18, S2, 7,
16, 17.   a,d—W   b,c—B   [Plate 63]

34. W B3, 14, 15, 16, 19, C2, 3, 4, 15, 17, 18, D4, 18,
E3, 17, F3, 17, G2, 3, N17, O17, P2, 4, Q2, 6,
16, 17, R3, 7, 18, S3, 6, 18.

B A3, 5, B4, 6, 13, 17, 18, C5, 13, 14, 16, D2, 3,
5, 15, 16, 17, E2, 4, 5, 14, F2, N3, O2, 3, P3,
18, Q3, 15, 18, R4, 5, 15, 17, S4, 17.

a,d—W   b,c—B   [Plate 64]

35. W A4, B5, 13, 14, 15, C5, 7, 15, 18, D2, 3, 5, 16,
17, 18, E3, 4, O2, 4, P2, 4, Q2, 3, 5, 11, 12, 13,
R5, 7, 11, 14, 15, S4, 16, T14.

B B3, 4, 12, 16, C2, 4, 12, 13, 14, 16, 17, D4, 6,
15, E5, 6, 15, F2, 4, G3, M3, N2, 3, O3, P3,
Q4, 14, 15, R3, 4, 12, 13, 16, 17, 18, S11, 13.

a,d—W   b,c—B   [Plate 65]

36. W B4, 6, 15, 16, C4, 7, 14, 17, D1, 2, 3, 17, E2, 18,
F2, L15, 17, M14, 18, N14, 18, O15, 16, P16,

18, Q2, 3, 12, 16, 18, R4, 6, 10, 12, 15, 16, 18
S2, 4, 11, 15, 18.

B   B3, 17, C1, 2, 3, 6, 16, D4, 6, 16, E4, 16, F17,
G2, 3, 17, N3, 12, 15, 16, 17, O3, 14, 17, P4,
12, 14, 17, Q4, 17, R2, 3, 13, 14, 17, S1, 3, 12,
16, 17.   a,b—W   c,d—B   [Plate 66]

37. W   B15, 16, C3, 5, 13, 14, 17, D4, 6, 17, E2, 3, 18,
L17, N17, O3, 17, P4, 17, Q4, 15, 16, R2, 3,
15, 17, 18, S3.

B   B17, C2, 15, 16, D2, 3, 14, E4, 15, 17, F4, 17,
G3, 17, O18, P18, Q2, 3, 17, 18, R4, 6, 13, 14,
16, S4, 15, 16.

a,d—W   b,c—B   [Plate 67]

38. W   B12, 13, 14, 15, 19, C15, 16, 18, D2, 3, 17, 18,
E4, 19, F4, 18, G4, 17, H3, J3, L17, M18, N17,
O17, P3, 4, Q2, 4, 6, 14, 15, 16, 17, R2, 7, 14,
18, S3, 6, 18.

B   B11, 16, 17, 18, C4, 6, 11, 12, 13, 14, 17, D4,
16, E2, 3, 14, 16, 17, 18, G2, 3, N3, 18, O2, 18,
P2, 18, Q3, 18, R3, 4, 5, 13, 15, 16, 17, S13, 14.
a,d—W   b,c—B   [Plate 68]

5. To rescue certain weak stones.

39. W   C2, 3, 5, 6, 11, 12, 13, 14, 18, D14, 17, E7, 18,
G3, 5, 17, H3, 5, K14, 16, 18, L18, M13, N5,
13, 15, O4, 6, 16, P4, 14, 17, Q3, 8, R3, 8, S3,
4, 7, 9.

B   B10, C9, 16, 17, D3, 5, 10, 13, 15, E5, 11, 14,
F3, 6, 13, 16, G6, J4, 7, K3, 6, M16, 18, N6, 14,
17, P5, 6, 8, 9, Q14, 15, 16, R4, 6, 7, 10, 11, 17,
S5.   a—B   b,c,d—W   [Plate 69]

40. W A2, B2, 5, 13, 17, C6, 13, 17, D3, 13, 16, 17,
E5, 7, 17, F5, 17, G2, 3, M2, 3, 13, 15, N11,
O10, 15, P2, 3, 13, Q9, 14, R2, 3, 4, 10, 15, S5,
6, 12, 16.

     B B15, C1, 2, 3, 4, 10, 14, 16, D4, 11, E14, 16,
F12, 14, G5, H2, 3, 4, N4, O12, 17, P4, 12, Q2,
3, 4, 6, 16, R5, 11, 12, 13, 17, S2, 3, 13, 17.

a,d—B   *b,c*—W   [*Plate 70*]

41. W B2, 3, C2, 4, 12, 17, D6, 9, 14, 18, E10, 12, 13,
17, F4, 7, 17, G3, 5, 15, H3, 5, 12, 14, 17, J6,
17, K5, 17, L4, N15, O15, 17, P17, Q8, 9, R3,
4, 5, 10, 11, 12, S2.

     B C3, 8, 9, 14, 15, 16, D2, 3, 10, E3, 5, 15, 16, F3,
13, 14, G4, J4, 5, 16, K4, 14, 16, L3, M3, 14,
16, N16, O13, P3, 5, 7, 8, 9, Q2, 5, 10, 14, 17,
R2, 7, 16, S1.

a,b—W   *c,d*—B   [*Plate 71*]

42. W B2, 4, 15, C2, 5, 8, 9, 13, 15, D10, 11, 13, 15,
E6, F4, 12, 13, G4, H3, 5, J5, K5, 15, 17, 18,
L4, 14, M7, 14, N6, 9, 16, 17, O4, 9, 14, P8,
10, 13, 16, Q3, 4, 6, 7, 8, 10, 17, R3.

     B B17, C1, 11, 12, 16, D2, 3, 4, 9, 12, 17, E9, 14,
F3, 10, 11, 14, 16, G3, 12, 13, J4, K4, L3, 18,
M3, 15, 16, 17, N15, O8, P5, 6, 7, Q5, 9, 15, 16,
R4, 5, 10, 11, 17, 18.

a,b,d—B   *c*—W   [*Plate 72*]

6. The Robber's Play.

43. W A16, B3, 13, 15, 17, 18, C1, 3, 4, 5, 6, 14, 19,
D2, 16, 17, 18, E3, 13, 16, F2, 16, G14, 15, N5,
O4, P3, 4, 6, 18, Q2, 15, 16, 17, R2, 7, 17, 18,
S3, 4, 6, 17, T5.

B A3, B2, 4, 5, 6, 16, C2, 7, 15, 16, 17, 18, D7,
15, E4, 6, 15, F4, 15, 17, G2, 3, 16, 17, M4, N2,
4, O3, 17, 18, P1, 2, 14, 16, Q3, 5, 14, R3, 5,
14, 16, S5, 16, 18, T17.

a,d—W   b,c—B   [Plate 73]

44. W A3, 18, B4, 15, 17, C4, 14, 18, D3, 4, 14, 19,
E14, 18, F2, 3, 4, 15, 18, G19, H16, 17, 18, P5,
6, Q3, 4, 9, 16, 17, 18, R3, 9, 13, 14, 15, 16, 18,
S4, 5, 7, 8, 16, T6.

B A16, B3, 16, 18, C3, 5, 6, 16, D2, 15, 17, 18,
E2, 6, 17, F1, 17, G2, 4, 5, 17, 18, H3, N4, O17,
P2, 3, 4, 12, 15, 18, Q5, 13, 15, R4, 5, 6, 7, 8,
12, 17, S6, 13, 14, 15, 17, 18, T16.

a,d—W   b,c—B   [Plate 74]

45. W A3, 4, 9, 12, B4, 6, 8, 10, 11, 13, 14, 16, 17, C2,
3, 5, 8, 15, D1, 3, 9, 15, E3, 11, 13, 14, F3, G3,
H3, 17, J2, 3, 15, 18, L14, 15, M14, N15, 16,
17, O4, 6, 17, 18, P2, 3, 8, 17, Q9, 17, R4, 5,
6, 9, S3, 4, 7, 9, T7, 8.

B A18, B1, 2, 3, 9, 12, 18, C1, 4, 9, 10, 11, 12, 13,
14, 17, D2, 4, 14, 17, E2, 4, 15, 16, F2, 5, G2,
H2, 5, J1, K2, 3, 4, 17, L16, M15, 16, 18, N14,
18, O14, 19, P18, Q3, 4, 5, 6, 7, 15, 18, R3, 7,
8, 16, 17, S2, 6, 8, T2.

a,d—W   b,c—B   [Plate 75]

46. W A15, B1, 2, 3, 4, 12, 13, 14, 16, C5, 11, 16, D4,
5, 11, 13, 17, E11, 14, 17, F2, 4, 15, G4, H3, 5,
J2, 3, 15, 16, 17, K15, L16, 17, 18, M15, 16, N15,
O3, 15, 17, P2, 15, 16, Q2, 9, 10, R3, 6, 7, 8,
10, S3, 4, 10.

B B5, 6, 10, 11, 15, C2, 3, 4, 6, 10, 12, 13, 14, 15,
D10, 15, 16, E3, F3, G2, 3, H2, J1, K2, 14, 16,

[129]

17, 18, L3, 14, 15, 19, M13, 17, 18, N16, 17, O13, 16, P17, 18, Q3, 5, 6, 7, 8, 14, R2, 4, 9, 16, S2, 9, T2.

a,d—W   b,c—B   [Plate 76]

47. W A3, 4, 13, 14, B2, 4, 12, 13, 15, 16, C4, 11, 13, 15, 17, 18, D3, 4, 12, E3, 18, F2, 3, 13, 15, 17, G3, 18, H3, K17, L17, M17, 18, N17, O17, P5, 6, 8, 16, Q3, 4, 10, 11, 16, R3, 11, 16, 17, S4, 5, 6, 8, 9, 11, 18, 19, T5, 7, 10.

B A12, B3, 6, 11, 14, C2, 3, 5, 14, 16, D1, 2, 13, 14, 15, 16, 17, 18, 19, E2, 5, F1, 5, G2, H2, 4, J3, 5, 16, 17, K18, L16, 18, M15, 19, N18, O15, 16, 18, P2, 3, 4, 17, Q5, 17, 18, R4, 5, 6, 7, 8, 9, 10, 18, S7, 10.

a,d—W   b,c—B   [Plate 77]

48. W A16, B1, 2, 3, 15, 17, 18, C4, 14, 19, D5, 17, 18, E5, 14, 17, F3, 4, 15, 16, 18, G3, H2, 3, 4, P6, Q6, 9, 14, 15, 16, 17, R4, 5, 10, 14, 18, S6, 7, 9, 18, T8, 18.

B B16, C2, 3, 16, 17, 18, D3, 16, E3, 4, 16, F2, 5, 17, G2, 6, 17, 18, H1, J2, 5, K3, O17, P18, Q3, 4, 5, 18, R2, 6, 7, 8, 12, 13, 15, 16, 17, S3, 8, 14, 17.   *a,d—W   b,c—B*   [Plate 78]

49. W A10, B6, 9, 11, C5, 8, 9, 11, 15, D5, 7, 11, 14, E12, 13, G3, H3, 17, J4, 16, K2, 3, 4, 16, 17, 18, L4, 6, 16, M15, N4, 5, O5, 10, 14, 15, P3, 4, 6, 7, 9, Q9, R5, 8, 11, S5, 8, 10, 11, 13, T9.

B B10, C6, 10, 12, D8, 9, 10, 12, E3, 6, 7, 11, F4, 11, 17, G16, H4, 5, 16, J2, 3, 17, 18, K1, 19, L2, 3, 17, 18, N3, 17, O3, 4, 16, P2, 15, Q2, 7, 8, 10, 11, 12, 17, R7, 9, 10, S6, 9.

a,d—W   b,c—B   [Plate 79]

7. To dismember a loose enemy chain.

50. W C15, D17, 18, E15, 17, G18, H18, J3, 13, K5, 6,
13, 14, 15, 16, 17, 18, L3, 4, 7, P3, 5, 7, Q2, 3,
9, R6.

B E18, F12, 17, 18, G13, 15, 17, H12, J11, 14, L5,
8, 12, 16, 18, M3, 8, 14, 16, N3, 5, 7, 18, O3,
8, P2.   *a,b—W*   *[Plate 80]*

51. W C15, D18, E13, 15, 16, 17, H5, 7, 9, 10, 18, J3,
12, 15, 17, K3, 5, 7, 9, 13, 14, 15, 17, L2, 3, M2,
9, O4, 6, 7, 8, Q3, R3.

B E18, F12, 13, 17, 18, G5, 6, 7, 9, 15, 17, H3, 4,
8, 12, 13, J2, 11, 14, L12, 16, 17, M3, 5, 7, 14,
N2, 3, 5, 7, P2, Q2.

a—W   *b—B*   *[Plate 81]*

52. W C15, D18, E13, 15, 16, 17, F13, H9, 10, 18, J3,
K3, 5, 7, 13, 14, 15, 16, 17, 18, L8, M9, O4, 5,
6, 9, P2, Q4.

B E18, F12, 17, 18, G3, 5, 7, 9, 15, 17, H3, 8, 12,
13, J16, K11, 12, L13, 18, M3, 5, 7, 15, 17, N3,
5, 7, O3.   *a—W*   *b—B*   *[Plate 82]*

Solutions

(The plays which are presented below exhibit exceptional elegance.)

1. **a.** T19. **b.** T2, S1, T4, Q2, R1. **c.** A18, A16, B16. **d.** B2, C1, B1, D1, C2.

2. **a.** O18, N18, Q17, R18, P18, N17, R17, O19, R19, P19, T17, *or* O18, P18, R18, *or* O18, R18, P18. **b.** S2, R1, S1. **c.** C17, C18, D17, E17, **B18,** D18, A18, B19, A12, A14, B14. **d.** A2, B1, A4, *or* A2, A4, B1.

3. **a.** T16, T18, T14, *or* T16, S12, T18. **b.** S5, S6, T5. **c.** A17, B19, B18, A14, C19, A16, A19, B17, B16. **d.** B1, A2, B2.

4. **a.** S18, S19, S13, T18, S15, T17, T14, *or* S18, S13, T16. **b.** S5, T5, T4, S4, T2, T6, Q2, *or* S5, T5, T4, S4, T2, Q2, S3, T4, T6, T4, T5, S1, S8. **c.** B19. **d.** C1.

5. **a.** Q15, Q14, R15, S15, T16, S14, Q19, T17, S18, N19, R19. **b.** T3, S6, T5, S3, R3. **c.** F17, G17, F18, G18, D18, E18, **D19,** E19, D16, F19, **B19,** A18, B18, A17, D14, C18, **B17,** C19, B16, *or* F17, G17, F18, G18, D18, E18, D19, E19, D16, F19, B19, C18, B18. **d.** A3, B1, B2, E3, A1, A2, C1.

6. **a.** T17, S15, R19. **b.** S1, T2, T3, P1, Q1, Q2, Q3, R1, R2. **c.** A16, A17, A15, B18, B19, B17, A18, A19, C19. **d.** C3, B3, B2, B1, A2, A3, B6, B5, A5, A1, D4, B4, B8, E1, B9.

7. **a.** T18, R18, R19, Q19, S19, T19, S19, *or* T18, R18, R19, S19, Q19. **b.** P1, N2, S1. **c.** H18, D18, J15, H15, **K18,** L18, **K19,** J17, J19, M17, G18, H19, **F17,** F19, E19. **d.** F1, D1, D2, *or* F1, D2, D1.

8. **a.** S18, R17, T17, R18, T13, S14, T16, T14, T11. **b.** R1, M1, P1, N1, Q2, *or* R1, P4, P1, Q2, Q3, M1, N1, O2,

O3, P2, *or* R1, O3, O2, P1, P2, P4, Q3, Q1, M1, O1.
c. A17, A18, B19, D17, C17, B18, D19, F19, C19, G19,
H19, H18, D18, A16, F18, J19, F17, *or* A17, A18, B19,
F19, C19, D19, D17, G19, D18. **d.** A2, B1, E2, A4, A3,
A1, A3, A5, C1.

9. **a.** G18, F18, G19, D17, K18, J19, J18, F19, J15, H18, K19,
   H19, L17, M16, M18, L18, N18, L16, M19, *or* G18, F18,
   G19, J18, E18, E17, D17, D18, E16, E19, F19, *or* G18,
   F18, G19, D17, K18, J19, J18, F19, J15, H18, K19, H19,
   L17, L18, L16, L15, M16, N18, N16, L14, N17, M18,
   O18, P18, O17, O19, N19, M19, L19. **b.** D2, E2, **D1,**
   F2, C6, C7, B7, C8, B4, B3, B1, B2, A4, A3, G2, *or*
   D2, E2, D1, F2, C6, C7, B7, C8, B4, B3, B1, E1, A4,
   C2, C1, B2, B8, *or* D2, E2, D1, C2, F2, C1, G5, G6, F1,
   E1, H1.

10. **a.** T16, R18, S19, R19, S18, S17, R17, T19, T17, Q19,
    S18. **b.** N2, N1, P1, O1, L1. **c.** E19, C18, J18, H18, H19.
    d. B7, C7, C6, B8, A5, A7, **B1,** A3, F5, G5, E7, A4, A2,
    B2, C2, A1, C1.

11. **a.** T12, T14, **S10,** R10, T10. **b.** **L2,** K2, L1, M3, M1, K3,
    O2, N1, P3, P1, Q1, *or* L2, K2, L1, M3, M1, K3, O2,
    P3, N1, P1, Q1, P2, N4. **c.** C17, B17, C16, B16, B18,
    C15, **B19,** A18, F15, H19, F17, F19, G19, E19, F18.
    d. B7, B6, **A7,** B8, A5, A6, C5, B5, D4, *or* B7, B6, A7,
    C5, A6, A5, A4, B4, B5.

12. **a.** P17, P18, N18, O18, N17, N16, O19, M18, N19, *or*
    P17, O18, T18, P18, S19. **b.** L1, J1, R1, K1, P1, N1, L2.
    c. B7, A9, B5, B6, A5, A7, B3.

13. **a.** S18, S17, S16, T16, T18. **b.** Q1. **c.** **D19,** G19, F19,
    F18, F17, E19, E18. **d.** A6, C6, B6.

14. **a.** S19, S18, R18, T19, T17, O19, T18. **b.** S1, T2,

T3, S2, P1, P2, Q1, R2, N1. **c.** A14, B13, A16, B12, C12, A11, A12, A13, B14. **d.** A2, E2, C2, F1, B1.

15. **a.** Q19, S18, T17, T16, R19, S19, T18, P19, Q19. **b.** S2, Q4, O5, R3, R1, S1, T1, S3, T4, T3, S4, *or* S2, R1, R4, R3, Q4, S4, S3. **c.** B19, C19, C18, A19, A17. **d.** A1, D1, B1.

16. **a.** S18, R18, S19, R19, S17, R17, S15. **b.** T5, T4, R4, S4, S2, S3, T2. **c.** C14, E18, C18, E17, B17, C16, A17, A16, B19, *or* C14, C18, E18, B18, C16, C17, A16, A15, A17, B15, C19, B19, A18, *or* C14, C18, E18, C16, B19, C19, B18, B15, A15. **d.** B1, B2, A1, E1, C1.

17. **a.** R19, P14, O13, O17, N18, R17, P19. **b.** T2, T5, T3, Q1, S2, R3, S1, *or* T2, T5, T3, S2, Q1, R1, T1. **c.** A15, A17, D18, C16, A16, B16, B18, *or* A15, B16, D18. **d.** B2, A2, C2, D1, A4, A3, A5, B3, B1, D4, C1, *or* B2, B3, C2, D1, A2, B1, A4, A3, D4.

18. **a.** Q19, R18, S15. **b.** S5, S4, S6. **c.** D18, D17, B17, B16, B18, C16, B15, A16, E19, C18, D19, *or* D18, D17, B17, B18, B16, G18, C18, B19, E18, D19, A18, F18, G19, *or* D18, C18, D17, C16, D16, B15, A14, A16, C19, B19, A18, A17, A13, B18, B16, B17, A15. **d.** B1, B2, E1, B4, B5, A4, A2.

19. **a.** S17, S16, S19, R18, S18, T18, T17, T16, Q19, R19, P19. **b.** S3, S2, S4, T2, O2, P1, R1, R2, S1. **c.** L18, G18, H19, D18, E19, *or* L18, D18, F18, G18, F17, E18, H18. **d.** F1, D1, A3, A2, B1, C1, G1, B2, D2, C2, E1.

20. **a.** S18, Q16, Q19, R19, R18, P19, S19, Q19, O19, *or* S18, R18, Q16, T18, S19, T16, Q19, R19, S17. **b.** Q2, Q1, R2, P3, T4, R5, P5, Q5, R3, P1, R4. **c.** B13, D10, B14, A18, A19, A15, C12, B12, D13, D11, D14, *or*

B13, C18, A19, E11, D10, D11, F11. **d.** G2, A2, D1, *or* G2, F2, A2, D2, C1, B1, E1, F1, D1.

21. **a.** S18, T17, R17, R18, T18, Q17, T16, R17, P18. **b.** R1, N2, O3, O1, M1, M2, Q1, L2, N1, L1, N1, M1, T3, T2, T4. **c.** B19, B18, E19, C18, B15.

22. **a.** P18, Q18, P19, M17, M19, L19, P17, Q16, N19, *or* P18, Q18, P19, N19, L19, S18, T18, M17, M19, M18, P17, Q16, O18, K19, L19, S19, Q19, O19, R16. **b.** T4, T3, S3. **c.** D19, C17, D17, A18, B17, B16, C16, B18, A16. **d.** D1, E2, E1, F1, C2.

23. **a.** T18, T17, S18. **b.** R3, Q3, Q1, S3, S1, R1, R2. **c.** B19, C19, B16, B17, A17, A16, A18. **d.** A2, A4, C2, C1, D2, E1.

24. **a.** S18, T16, T17. **b.** P1, O2, T2, T3, Q2, Q3, R3, S2, R1, T1, N2, *or* P1, Q1, Q3, Q2, S2, T2, S1, R3, O2, *or* P1, S2, O2, Q1, S6, S8, R5, R8, Q3, Q2, T3, T2, S1. **c.** A18, C19, B19. **d.** D1, B2, B3, A3, A2, A1, B1.

25. **a.** T18, S18, P19, T19, Q19. **b.** S2, T4, T3. **c.** B18, D19, C19. **d.** A2, B2, A3, E1, B1.

26. **a.** P19, T17, T18, S19, R19, R18, Q18, *or* P19, R19, S19, S18, T18, *or* P19, S18, T18, R18, Q18, R19, S19. **b.** R1, S1, T1. **c.** A18, A17, B19. **d.** C3, C2, B1, A2, E1, F1, F2, E2, G1, A4, C1, D1.

27. **a.** T18, R18, S19, R19, P19, P17, T17. **b.** S3, S2, T2, S4, T4, *or* S3, S2, T2, R2, S8. **c.** A16, B16, A15, A17, A18, A19, B19, *or* A16, B16, A15, B15, A18, B19, B17.

28. **a.** R18, R16, S19, T18, T17, P19, Q19. **b.** Q3, P2, S5. **c.** B14, B13, B18, A14, A17, C18, A15, B15, B16. **d.** C1, D2, A1.

29. **a.** S15, Q15, S18, S19, T16, T13, T14. **b.** P2, O2, O1,

N2, Q1, Q2, O4, P3, T2, *or* P2, Q2, O3, O4, N2, N1, O1, *or* P2, O2, O1, N1, P3, P4, O3, O4, N2. **c.** D18, B19, C19. **d.** B1, C1, C2.

30. **a.** R18, R15, Q19, *or* R18, S19, Q19. **b.** G4, F1, H1, J2, G1, E2, H2, H3, F2, *or* G4, F1, H1, J1, E2, D1, C1, E1, H2, H3, J2, K2, K1, L1, L2, *or* G4, E1, F2. **c.** A17, A13, A15, D17, A19, *or* A17, A,15, B15.

31. **a.** L19, Q18, P19, N18, Q19, L18, K18, M19, M18. **b.** T4, T2, S1, Q2, R2, S2, Q1, *or* T4, S2, Q2, Q3, Q1, R1, S1, *or* T4, Q2, S2, T3, O1, S1, R1, T2, T1. **c.** B18, B15, D18, C18, C19, E18, C17. **d.** D2, C3, C2, B2, B3, B4, A3, A4, C4, A2, B3, A3, D4, B3, B1, B5, B6, A6, B7, E1, A7.

32. **a.** T18, T19, S15, S16, R17, S17, R18, Q17, R18, R17, S19, *or* T18, R17, Q17, R18, T19, S15, T15, R15, T17. **b.** T3, T5, T4, R5, S5. **c.** C19, B19, A16, A15, B17, B16, A18. **d.** H3, K2, B3, B2, A2, A3, B1.

33. **a.** S19. **b.** S4, R4, R5, T4, T2, T3, T6. **c.** B18, D19, B19, C19, F19. **d.** B1.

34. **a.** T18, R19, R16, S16, S15, S14, P17. **b.** S2, R2, T3. **c.** A18. **d.** B1, A2, F1.

35. **a.** T12, T11, S10. **b.** S2, S3, R2, T2, S1. **c.** A16, A17, B18. **d.** B2, A2, B1, C1, C3, A1, B2, B1, A5.

36. **a.** T12, S13, T15, T13, O18. **b.** T2, T3, Q1, P2, R1, T1, S2. **c.** B18, C18, B19. **d.** A4, B5, **B1**, A2, F3, *or* A4, A5, C5, B5, B7, A3, A2, B1, A4.

37. **a.** S17, T18, T16, S14, Q19, T17, N18, S18, R19, *or* S17, S19, S14, S13, R19, Q19, T17, T18, N18. **b.** S1, R1, T3. **c.** B18, C18, B19. **d.** B2, B3, C4, B1, A2, A3, D1, A1, B2, A2, E1.

38. **a.** S15, S16, S17. **b.** S2, S1, T2, T3, Q1, T1, S2, T2, P1.

   c. A18, A16, A15, A14, A12. d. B2, B3, C2, F3, F1.
39. a. O15, N16, M15, O14, O17, *or* O15, P15, P18, Q18, P16, O17, O18, Q17, O14. b. T5, T6, S6, T4, Q5, Q6, P7, O7, O5, Q7, R5, Q4, R5, Q5, T3. c. E15, E16, B17, B16, D16, C15, A16. d. F5, E6, E2, F2, E4, D4, E3, D2, D1.

40. a. S15, T15, S14, R16, Q15, R14, P14. b. Q1, S4, R1, O3, N1, O2, O1. c. A15, A16, B16, A14, C15. d. F4, E4, F3, E3, F2.

41. a. L16, M15, M18, L18, M17, L17, L19. b. S8, S7, T7, R8, Q7, S9, R9, R6, T8, Q6, T5, *or* S8, S7, T7, R8, Q7, R9, S9, T6, Q6. c. F12, F11, D11, E11, B17, B18, B11, B12, A12, B13, B14, A13, D12. d. J2, H2, H1, J3, K3, H4, G1, F2, F1.

42. a. N18, O18, O19, P18, O16, O17, O15, P15, P19, *or* N18, P18, P19, O18, O16. b. S7, S8, R8, R7, R9, S6, P9, R6, T7. c. E12, E13, B12, B11, E11, C10, A11, E10, A9. d. J2, H2, H1, J3, K3, K2, J1, G1, H4, K1, J1.

43. a. T18, T19, R19. b. S2, S1, T2, T3, Q1, T1, S2. c. B19, A19, A17, A15, E18. d. A2, A1, A4, A5, D1.

44. a. T15, T14, T18, S19, T17, T19, T17, T18, R19, S11, T17, S17. b. S3, S2, R2, T3, Q2, S3, T5, Q8, T7, S9, S1, Q7, T2. c. B19, C19, C17, A19, B18, B19, A17. d. C2, B2, B1, C1, A2.

45. a. M17, L17, N19, M19, L18, K18, K19, L19, J19. b. T3, S5, T4. c. B15, A15, A13, A14, A17. d. H1, G1, E1, F1, D1.

46. a. J18, K19, N19, O19, J19. b. S5, R5, Q4, S6, T3, T5, T4. c. A14, A13, C17, B17, A16, A17, A11. d. D3, D2, E2, E1, D1, F1, E2, F2, C1.

47. **a.** N19, O19, Q19. **b.** S3, S2, T3, T2, R2, T4, S3, T3, Q2, S3, S1, *or* S3, S2, T3, R2, T2, T1, S1, R1, Q1. **c.** B17, B18, A18, A17, A15, A16, B19. **d.** B1, K2, C1.

48. **a.** S15, T15, T17. **b.** S5, S4, T7, T6, T4. **c.** E19, D19, B19, A19, A17, A18, F19. **d.** E2, E1, G1, F1, D1, D2, C1.

49. **a.** H18, J19, M17, M18, L19, M19, H19, L19, N18, M16, N19. **b.** S7, T8, R13, T10, S12, R12, T12, T13, S14, T11, R14, *or* S7, T8, R13, S12, T10, T11, S14. **c.** B12, A11, B7, D6, A8. **d.** H2, J1, M3, M2, N2, M4, O2, M3, L1.

50. **a.** G16, F16, G14, F14, F15. **b.** N6, M6, O6, M7, M4.

51. **a.** G16, F16, G14, H15, F15. **b.** K6, J6, L6, J8, J4.

52. **a.** G16, F16, G14, H14, H15, *or* G16, H16, H14, G14, F16. **b.** J4, K4, K6, J6, L6, *or* J4, H4, K4.

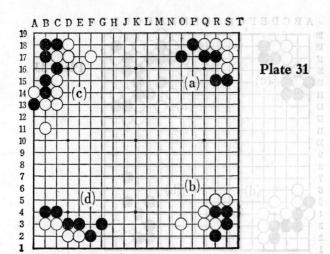

Plate 31

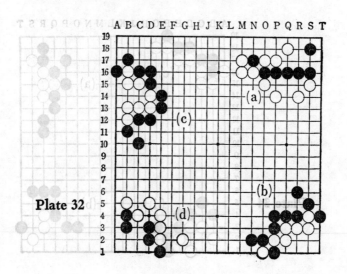

Plate 32

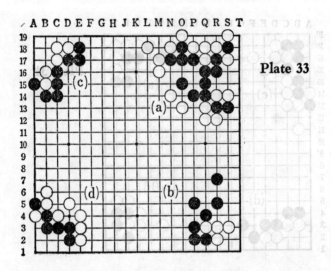

Plate 33

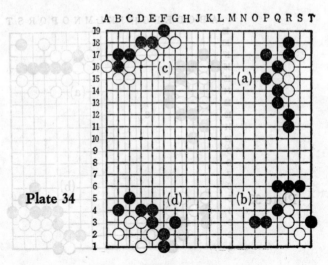

Plate 34

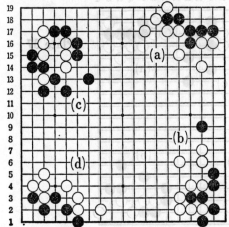

Plate 35

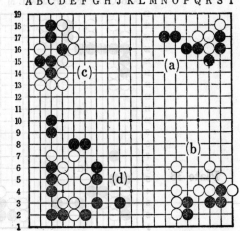

Plate 36

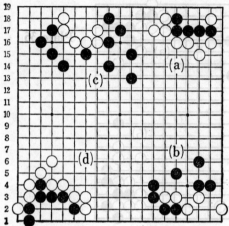

Plate 37

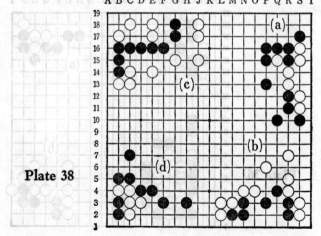

Plate 38

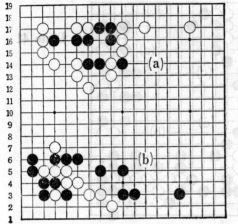

Plate 39

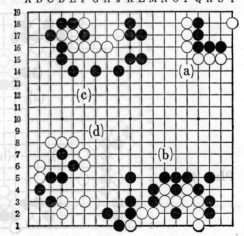

Plate 40

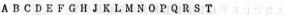

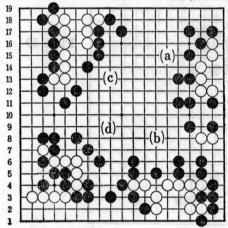

Plate 41

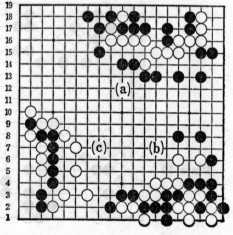

Plate 42

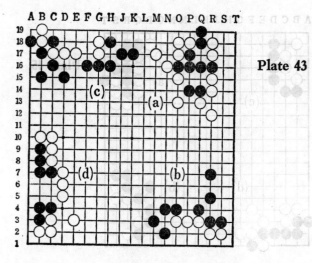

Plate 43

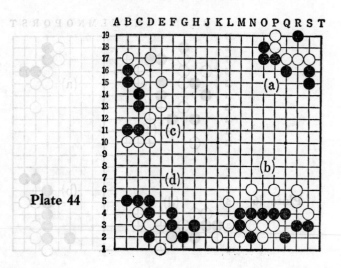

Plate 44

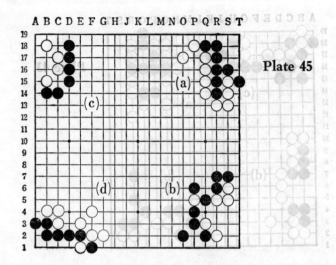

Plate 45

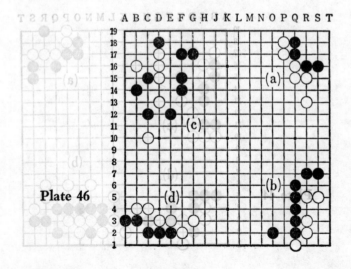

Plate 46

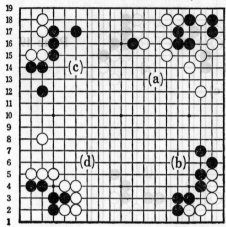

Plate 47

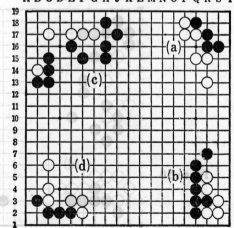

Plate 48

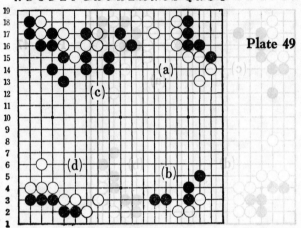

Plate 49

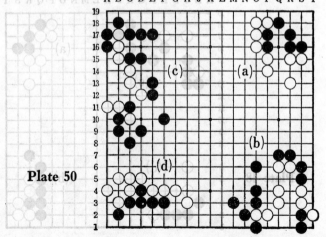

Plate 50

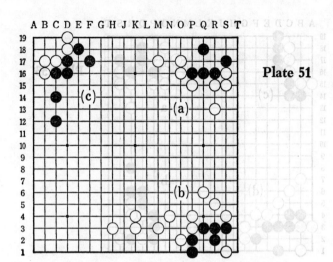

Plate 51

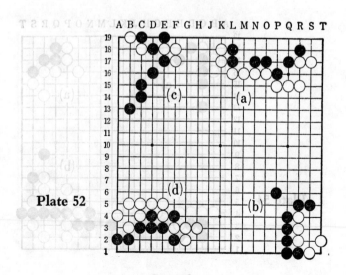

Plate 52

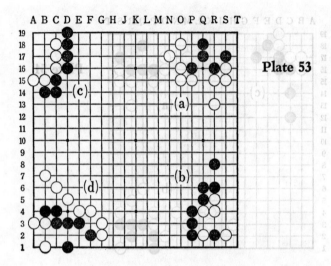

Plate 53

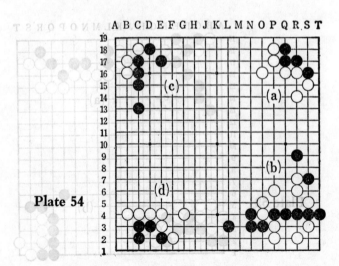

Plate 54

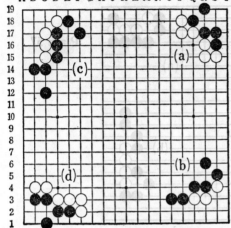

Plate 55

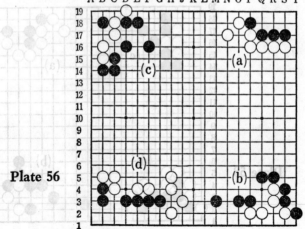

Plate 56

[151]

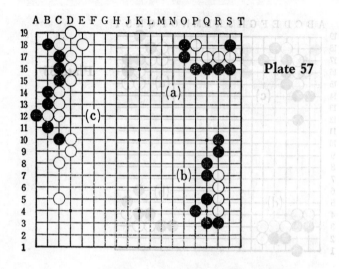

Plate 57

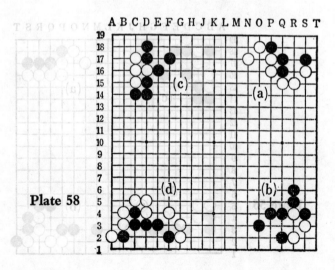

Plate 58

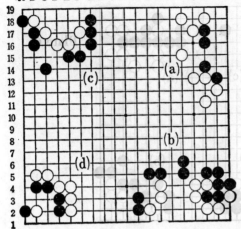

Plate 59

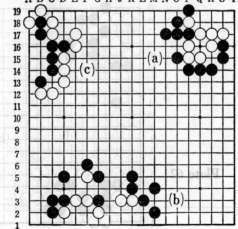

Plate 60

[153]

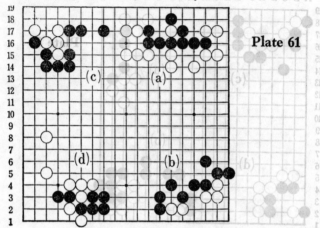

Plate 61

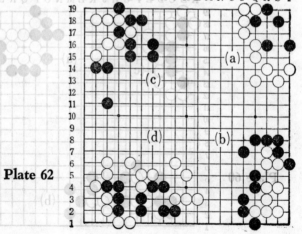

Plate 62

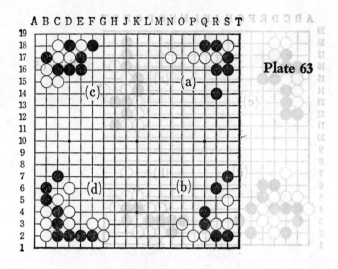

Plate 63

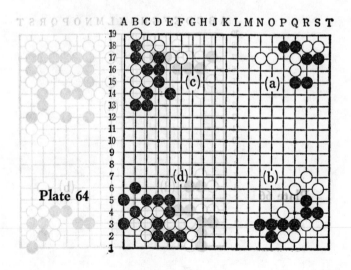

Plate 64

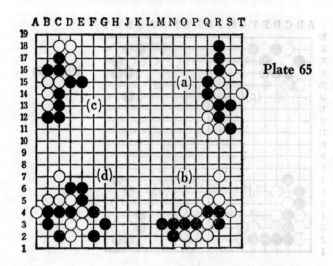

Plate 65

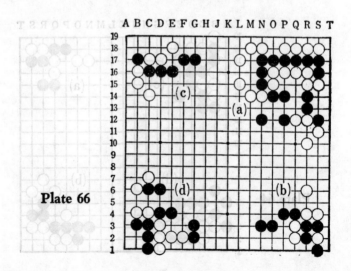

Plate 66

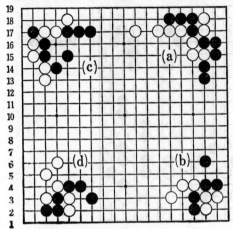

Plate 67

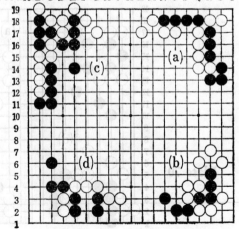

Plate 68

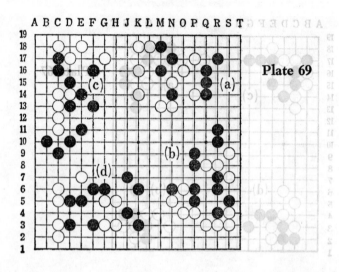

Plate 69

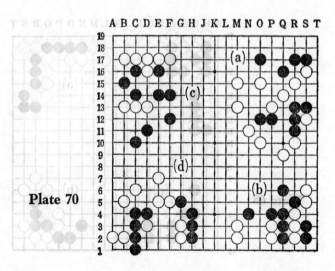

Plate 70

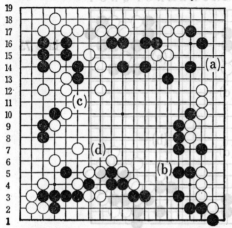

Plate 71

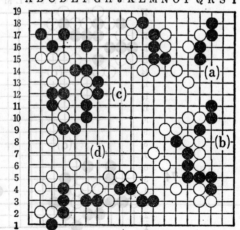

Plate 72

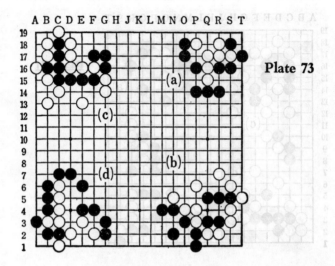

Plate 73

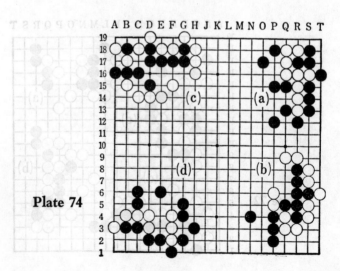

Plate 74

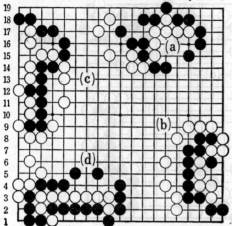

Plate 75

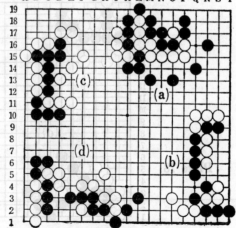

Plate 76

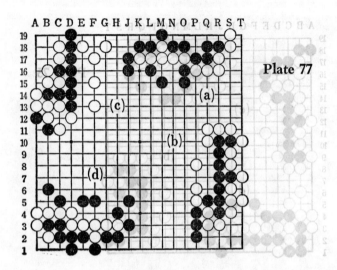

Plate 77

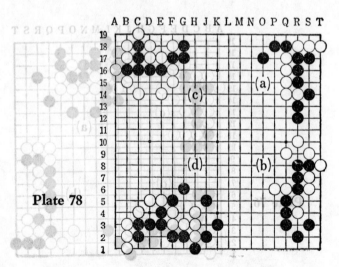

Plate 78

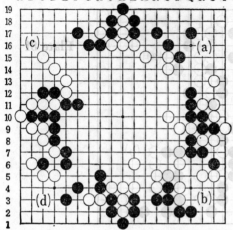

Plate 79

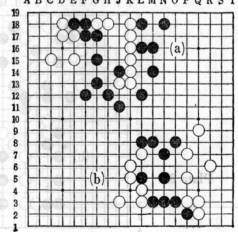

Plate 80

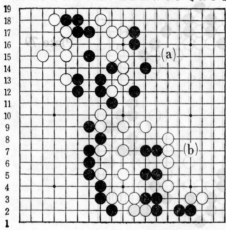

Plate 81

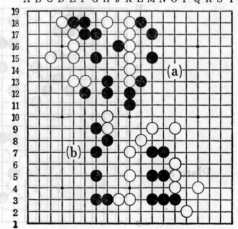

Plate 82

VI
End Plays

ANY GAME of *Go,* due to the possibilities structurally inherent in its moves, should, on the average, result in about 250 moves. Of the total sum, about 20 belong to the opening game, about 150 to the middle game, and, say, about 80 to the end game. Plays effecting the connection of chains at the margin and filling up the gaps and interspaces between the chains, after the general formation is completed, belong to the end game. The end game, however, is not in any precise way sharply distinguished from the middle game. Long before the middle game has reached its full development moves occur here and there that belong in kind to those characteristic of the end game. They become more and more frequent as the game progresses until finally only plays of the end game type are made.

The value that any play of the end game type has can always be estimated—in fact, usually to the exact eye. One should, therefore, make an overall survey of the board, as the end game moves toward its final stage, deciding upon and checking out the value of the future end plays, to see whether one will lose or gain Upperhand by means of a particular end play. If several end plays leading to Upperhand are possible, then one may, when necessary, gain Upperhand through a sacrifice related to the expected gain, and develop the end plays with Upperhand one after another according to the value of each position. But if Upperhand is not quite certain or if the opponent is aggressive and fond of taking the offensive and so not shy also at making a sacrifice to obtain Upperhand, then one may forego completing the end plays in their order of value, to assume first those plays which are, as conditioned by an opponent's attack, attended by the greatest safety.

But one will never be able to complete all the end plays where Upperhand is possible, without in due course alternately giving over Upperhand to an opponent, thus allowing him a chance to work at completing his sequence of end plays. Sooner or later a moment of the game will intervene making a major end play advantageous in which Upperhand is lost rather than pushing forward the sequence of end plays. This happens when more points can be won by giving away Upperhand than by keeping it, that is, when the maximum end play is worth more points with the loss of Upperhand than the maximum play with its retention. Thus the opponent eventually obtains Upperhand, but only in turn to give it up for the same reason.

With the repetitive shifting of Upperhand the value of the surviving plays decreases until finally only the insignificant stones *(Dame)* are left to be set out. Usually it makes little difference which player sets these out.

So much for the general scheme of an end game. In actual play, of course, many deviations must be made from such a skeletonic frame of reference. One often tries by what are basically aimless plays, actually superficial though apparently dangerous, to bluff. Or one may sometimes break away from a reasonable sequence intentionally to make a trivial end play, perhaps in an especially odd way, in order eventually to secure Upperhand by means of an adjoining end play. But more often deviations arise because each player has his own notion about the value of a particular end play, thus not retorting as expected to an attack. As a result Upperhand is shuffled back and forth more often than the strict logic of the game requires.

Among available Japanese publications there is only one work strictly concerned with the end game, called *Igo Shu Kai Roku* (or *Collection of End Games*), and written by Inouye Inseki XI.* Examples from this collection will prove useful for the learner.

The art of computing the value of end plays can be shown well enough by a few examples. With some drill, any player can then, with no great difficulty, himself reckon out all of the potential cases. Also, in most of the following examples, the first moves only are given, the remaining plays being obvious and therefore omitted.

---

*The eleventh head of the House of Inouye.

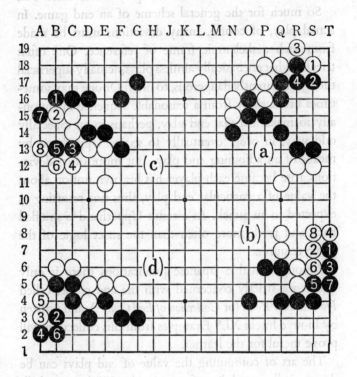

Plate 83

This always happens in practice when the corresponding end play signifies little or nothing.

As before, the diagrams (at most four) for each plate will be designated:

(c)	(a)
(d)	(b)

The abbreviations "U. R." and "U. L." mean "Upperhand Retained" and "Upperhand Lost," respectively.

1. *Plate 83.*

   Diagram (a). 6 points. U. R. In the present diagram the points Q19, S19, T17, 18, 19 are yet to be occupied. The 6 points involved in this example are S17, 18, 19, T17, 18, 19. These would have remained unoccupied, if Black had had Upperhand. Then the play would have been:

B	W
R19	Q19
R17	—

   Diagram (b). 5 points. U. R. A common situation. If it were White's Upperhand, we should have:

B	W
—	S5
T5	T6
T4	S7

   This makes a difference of 5 points (compare with diagram (b)), namely T4, which Black now loses, and S6, 8, T7, 8 which now remain open to White.

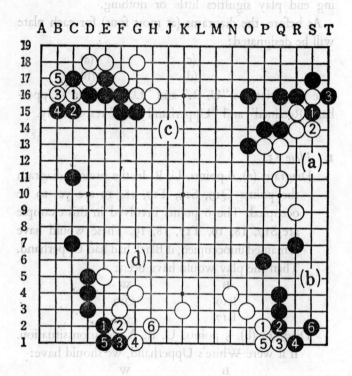

Plate 84

Diagram (c). Some 13 points. U. R. Common situation.

Diagram (d). 8 points. U. R.

2. *Plate 84.*

Diagram (a). 17 points, if *Ko* develops, otherwise 15 points. U. L. The 15 points are R17, 18, 19, S13, 14, 16 (doubled), 18, 19, T13, 14, 15, 17, 18, 19.

Diagram (b). 6 points. U. R.

Diagram (c). Somewhat more than 18 points. U. L.

Diagram (d). 6 points. U. R.

3. *Plate 85.*

Diagram (a). About 14 points. If S19 had been played previously, then it would be 9 points. U. L.

Diagram (b). 14 points. U. L. Good play technique.

Diagram (c). About 7 points. U. R.

Diagram (d). 12 points. U. L. Common situation.

4. *Plate 86.*

Diagram (a). 4 points. U. R.

Diagram (b). 2 points. U. R.

Diagram (c). 6 points. U. R. Common situation.

Diagram (d). This technique is good, though in spite of it Upperhand is lost.

5. *Plate 87.*

Diagram (a). 8 points. U. L.

Diagram (b). 10 points. U. L.

Diagram (c). 17 points. U. L. Good technique.

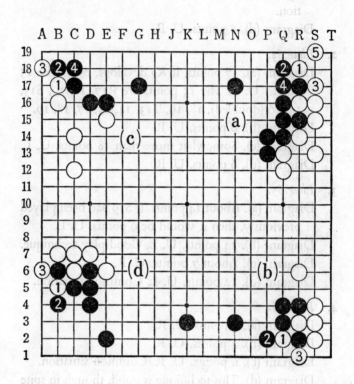

Plate 85

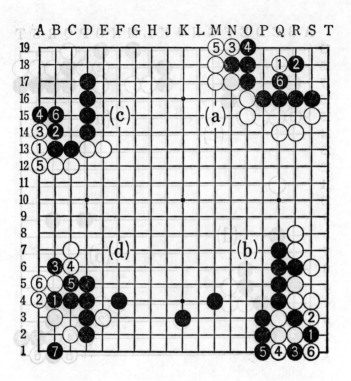

Plate 86

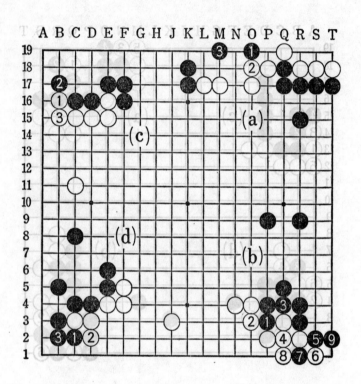

Plate 87

Diagram (d). 11 points. U. L. Play 1 C2 would have gone better at B2.

6. *Plate 88.*
   Diagram (a). 5 points. U. R. Common situation.
   Diagram (b). Some 10 points. U. R. Good technique.
   Diagram (c). 7 points. U. R.
   Diagram (d). 14 points. U. R.

7. *Plate 89.*
   Diagram (a). U. L. 1 O19 looks advantageous, but is not; should go to Q19.
   Diagram (b). The advantage is very significant. U. R.
   Diagram (c). 3 points. U. R.
   Diagram (d). Some 12 points. U. L.

8. *Plate 90.*
   Diagram (a). 3 points. U. R.
   Diagram (b). U. L. Play 5 S5 is worth some 14 points.
   Diagram (c). 8 points. U. L.
   Diagram (d). U. L. Profitable technique.

9. *Plate 91.*
   Diagram (a). 18 points. U. L.
   Diagram (b). $8\frac{1}{2}$ points. U. R.
   Diagram (c). About 12 points. U. R.
   Diagram (d). 18 points. U. L.

10. *Plate 92.*
    Diagram (a). About 9 points. U. R.
    Diagram (b). 9 points. U. R. (5 on G2, 6 on G3).

11. *Plate 93.*

Diagram (a). Some 9 points. U. R.

Diagram (b). 4 points. U. L.

Diagram (c). Some 12 points. U. L. Good technique.

Diagram (d). 16 points. U. L.

12. *Plate 94.*

Diagram (a). Some 12 points. U. L.

Diagram (b). $3\frac{1}{2}$ points. U. R.

Diagram (c). Some $7\frac{1}{2}$ points. U. L. Play 7 G19 is worth 4 points.

Diagram (d). 18 points. U. L. (6 on D3).

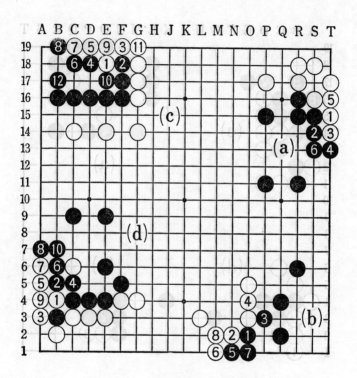

Plate 88

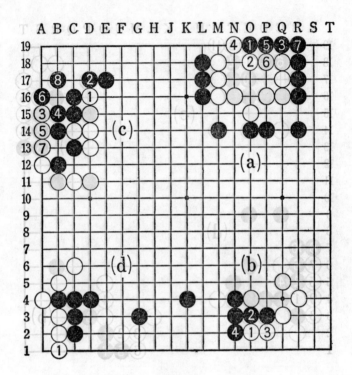

Plate 89

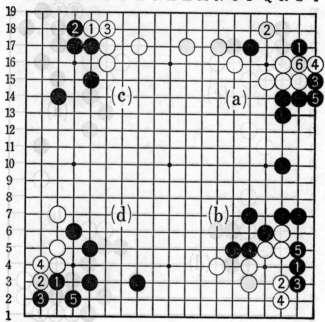

Plate 90

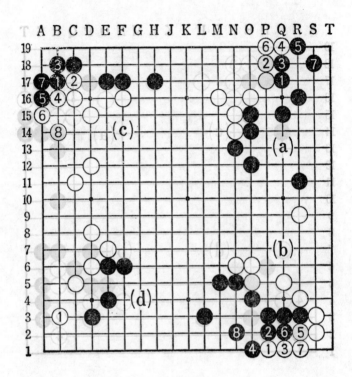

Plate 91

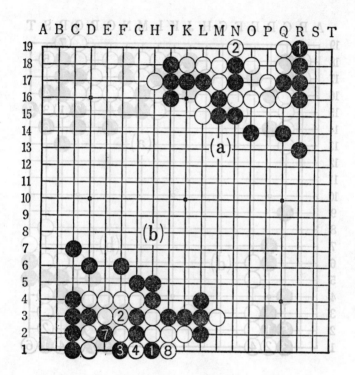

Plate 92

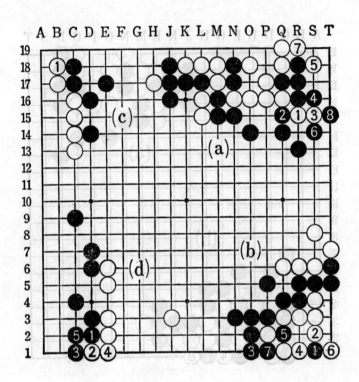

Plate 93

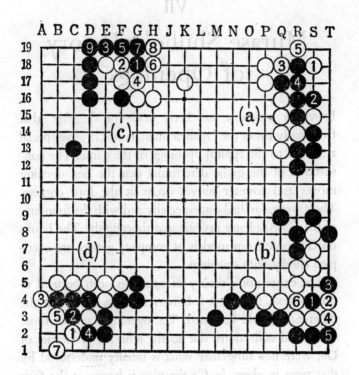

Plate 94

VII

Murase Shuho's Theory
of Openings

PREVIOUS MENTION has been made of the fact that from early times the Japanese masters of *Go* gave special attention to the typical openings of the game. The constitution of the game determines that the best opening moves and counter moves occur at the four corners. These were searched out especially and with the founding of the *Go* Academy investigated thoroughly. The books on *Go,* aside from models of complete games, are occupied chiefly with openings.

The expression "theory of openings" can be used in this context, though it is borrowed from chess. But the difference should be noted. The openings, at least those of the old collections, due to the inherent properties of *Go,* were not altogether what is usually understood by that term in chess. In *Go* the play is begun at the four corners, and there are, taken successively, four openings in contrast with one in chess. If a play is made at each corner, then the positions of the stones in the two adjacent corners begin to influence any further corner plays. As a result the number of possibilities, not only those already existing but those structurally imminent, is already of so great a magnitude, even after merely a few plays, that from any given formation the totality of good continuations defies analysis.

The *Go* masters of earlier times saved themselves from this complexity by a certain device. They studied the openings of each corner, taken one at a time, thus simplifying the situation. Limited to this device, one could, of course, use in an actual game only the first plays of the model openings. The remaining formulated plays could serve only to indicate in which direction the game might further develop if one disregarded the positions meanwhile arising at other corners. Of course, to foresee all the possibilities at once would be extremely useful. From such a position of advantage one could as each opportunity arose make use of it, partially at least, in the development of the game. The openings are not so numerous as in chess, as the matter stands, but must be more carefully studied. Plate 95, duplicated from a page of *Igo Myoden* (setting forth an outstanding style of play for *Go,* published in 1852 A.D. by Inouye Inseki XI), will make quite clear why a more careful study of *Go* openings is required than is the case in chess.

So far as I know, Hattori was the first to publish openings in our present sense, in his 10-volume work *Oki Go Ji Zai.* This handbook of openings appeared in the first part of this [the 19th] century. It is a "must" for anyone who wishes to learn advanced *Go.* This is so even if strictly speaking it has been outmoded by subsequent already of so great a magnitude, even after merely a few plays, that from any given formation the totality of good

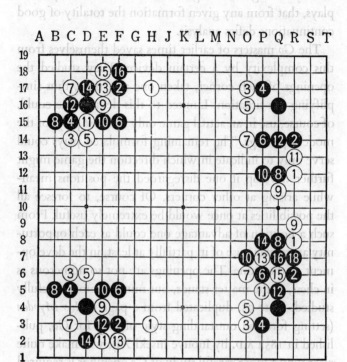

Plate 95

So far as I know, Hayashi was the first to publish openings in our present sense, in his to-volume work Oki Go Ji Zai. This handbook of openings appeared in the first part of this [the 19th] century. It is a "must" for anyone who wishes to learn advanced Go. This is so even if strictly speaking it has been outmoded by subsequent progress in technique. Since more recent works about openings have not been made public, I should have found it necessary to adapt material from Hattori's book for this chapter. But Murase Shuho allowed me, most kindly, to use his manuscript which contains a collection of openings, not to be published until later. Shuho (a master is usually referred to in *Go* documents by his given name) himself has selected the fifty openings, given below, for me. He has also contributed the elucidations about them. In a Japanese edition no notes are supplied except of the most abbreviated sort on the margins of the tables. The Japanese expect a reader to think a problem through for himself.

Shuho's openings exceed by far anything so far offered in *Go* handbooks. They determine a level of perfection for *Go* that can hardly be much exceeded. I must confess that I rarely enjoyed such exceptional pleasure as that afforded by the study of his openings. I am only concerned that perhaps none of my readers may be in a position to enjoy them fully. The charm of his examples must take instant hold upon anyone who works over them industriously. Still, to appreciate them in their full perfection a complete knowledge of all the available literature on *Go* is needed. A comparison with Hattori's technique as also with that of Inouye XI around 1840 A.D. shows at once the tremendous advance accomplished in *Go* by Shuho. Such a comparison will multiply the brilliance of the examples from Shuho given below.

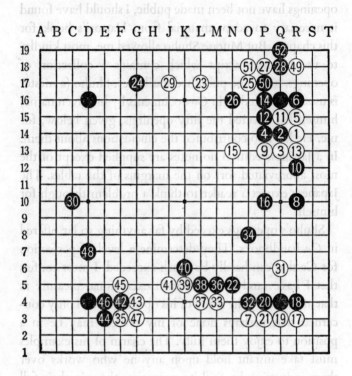

Plate 96

Among Shuho's predecessors the game is rigid, the combinations more modest in range. But with Shuho it is evident how free from clumsiness, imposed by the physical apparatus, the game has become. The plays are now wonderful in their free combinatorial possibility and in the precisely thought out order of steps. And, though his combinations are superlatively bold, they are also indubitably safe based as they are on a mastery of the game unprecedented in its scope. The excellent features of Murase's technique were already known through the games published in his magazine for *Go*. But, being half-obscured through his opponents' variously distributed plays, they did not stand out as distinctly as they do in the examples below.

One should be aware that in the examples below the plays assigned to Black are always the best possible. Thus White is constantly at a disadvantage except for a few cases. In these Murase allows Black to make a defective but still feasible play in order to show its harmful effect.

I. Black has a handicap of 4 stones.

1. *Plate 96.*

8. R10. Prior to this one might in this case play R7, which simultaneously retorts to O3 and (remotely) attacks R14, 15. One does better limiting himself to R10 in view of White's latter position.

16. P10. Better than R7.

18. R4. Better than Q3, which, it is true, separates O3

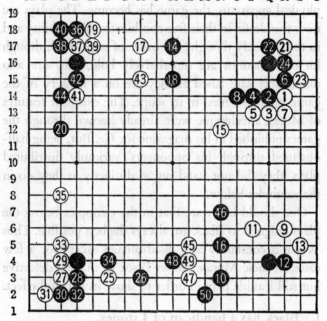

Plate 97

and R3; however, Black at R10 would then be weak.
28. Q18. Black is quite satisfied to have only two eyes
there, since he has that much more territory on the
left side.

33. M4. Better than O7, for then Black follows with
N3. Q6 is a *Sute Ishi*, a stone to be sacrificed. It forces
Black to 34 O8 and helps later to narrow the Black
position still more in that every attack from outside
through its presence on the inside becomes much more
telling, and it can also be used later in regard to *Ko*.
Black now plays 36 M5, 38 L5 and 40 K6 in order to
tone up his position rendered weak by Q6.

49. R18. A tyro would play S16 or Q17.

2.   *Plate 97.*

14. K17. Better than an attack with Q9, which was
formerly to be expected.
16. N5. Seems to me [Korschelt] very good.
22. Q17. Instead of

B	W
S15	P18
N18	S18

O7   and at the end of the game better
for Black by some 8 points, but very dangerous.

26. H3. On account of N3—N5, otherwise F4.
30. C2. Instead of which, too

B	W
D5	D2

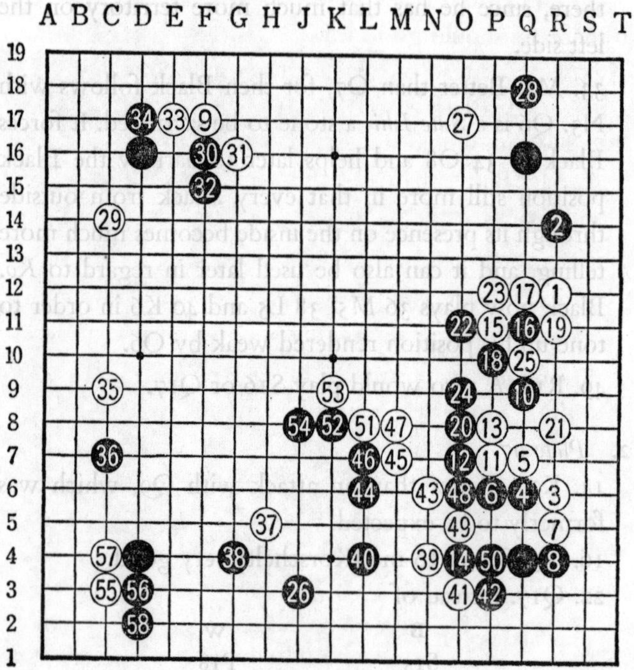

Plate 98

E2	C2
E3	C6 is equally good.

42. D15. If the Black position on K15—K17 were not there, 42 should go to C14.

43. H15. Instead of which C14 would be useless.

46. N7. If Black played 46 L3, then White N6 follows and White would have the advantage.

50. M2. Better than 50 P3 since it protects equally well and attacks at the same time.

3. *Plate 98.*

16. Q11. 16 P9 would be very bad.

39. N4. Destroys Black territory, but brings White no direct gain.

58. D2. Much better than C5. Note

B	W
C5	B5
B6	D5
C6	D2
E2	B2
F3	E9

The attack on White at M takes place better with 58 D2.

4. *Plate 99.*

10. G3. Could have played first

B	W
P3	O4
R6	—

28. Q6. The same as R6.

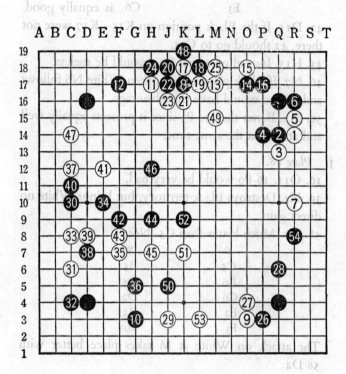

Plate 99

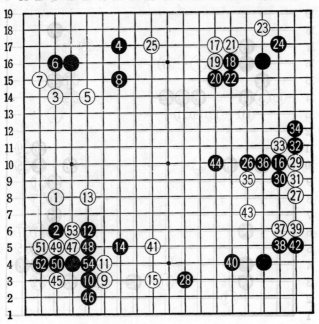

Plate 100

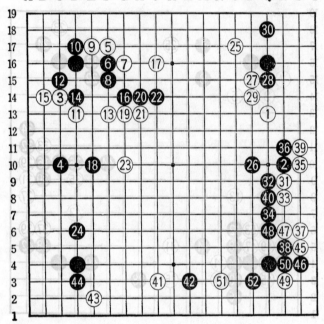

Plate 101

40. C11. Very important because it prevents the connection of C12 with C8 *(Watari).**

5. *Plate 100.*

27. S8. Particularly bad.

30. R9. If Black plays 30 S11, then 27 S8 would have been quite good.

47. D5. Indeed false, but is played to confuse Black and to bring about C5. White has given several stones as a handicap and is forced to make such tricky plays for which it is not easy to find a counter move. White expects that Black will make a faulty reply and thereby forfeit the superior advantage that he has through the four or more handicap stones.

6. *Plate 101.*

24. D6. A continuation of the pursuit of White brings no special gain.

31. R9. See the note to 47 D5 in example 5 above.

51. N3. 51 S3 would be false. Note

B	W
—	S3
Q3	T4
K5	—

7. *Plate 102.*

16. R6. R5 would also be good.

32. R16. Seems small but is in fact rich with implications.

---

*[*Watari* refers to tactics whereby two nearby emplacements are connected by a play between them. *Eds.*]

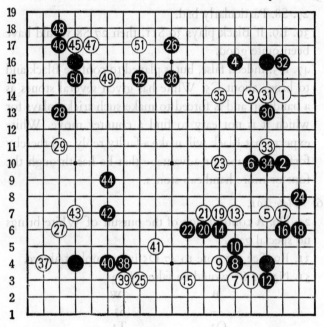

Plate 102

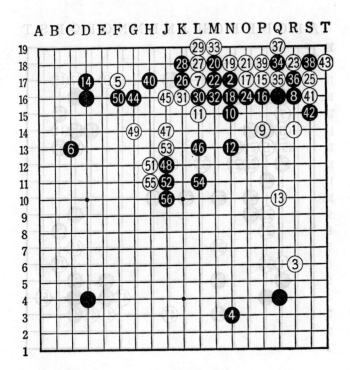

Plate 103

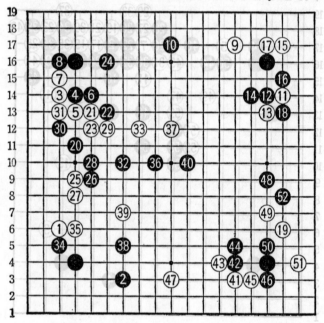

Plate 104

8. *Plate 103.*

14. D17. If Black were now to play M18, his position on the right would be unassailable. It should, however, be pointed out in this example that Black, if he had only defended himself properly, would have had no need for M18, and yet finally remain with the advantage.

9. *Plate 104.*

20. D11. Needed. With it the White position remains feeble.

52. R8. Better than S3.

10. *Plate 105.*

13. F12. Made possible by D7. If C6 were to be played instead of D7, then would come 13 D10.

15. B15. After 15 C10 would follow 16 B14 and the connection with the upper position would be accomplished.

42. L16. Also C5 is good.

II. Black has a handicap of 3 stones.

11. *Plate 106.*

8. M5. Also

B	W
L5	J3
M3	M2
M4	Q8

Q8 is played in order to obstruct Black's R5.

16. R11. Black cannot play R5 without suffering P3, 4 to be cut off.

Plate 105

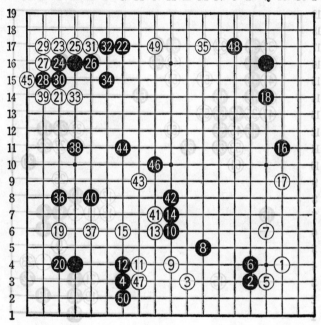

Plate 106

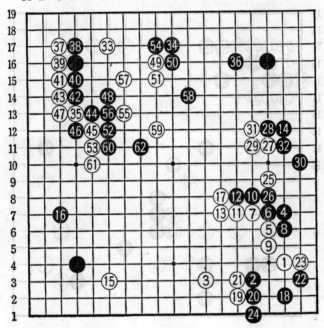

Plate 107

39. B14. For this Black A14 is the traditional retort. But this time Black cannot make that play, since White B12 would follow, whereby Black's C8—D11 would be too much threatened.

45. A15. Black cannot occupy A14 with either of his plays 42 or 44.

50. G2. To protect the Black position G2 is needed, and, besides, thereby Black does not lose Upperhand.

12.　*Plate 107.*

4. R7. Then usually follows

B	W
—	Q5
R10	O4
Q14	—

Here one should see how Black undertakes to cope with this unusual attack.

31. P12. Better than S9 because the six isolated Black stones can still break through towards the middle. With P12 White obtains a major front against that. This opening is outside the usual trend.

13.　*Plate 108.*

7. R5. R2 would be bad, for

B	W
R5	Q3*
S4	R3
Q5	P2
R9	and Black would have the advantage.

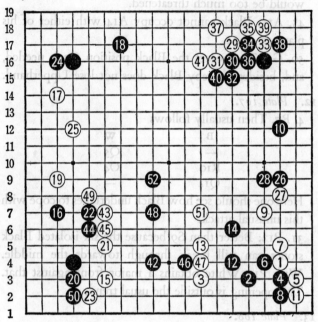

Plate 108

11. S2. Seems petty, but it seriously weakens the Black position.

23. E2. The importance of this play, if an extensive territory has only F3—F5 for covering protection on one side, has been referred to prior to this.

41. M16. A long established and well known opening.

42. J4. Since Black is safe at all points, he can undertake a bold attack.

14. *Plate 109.*

7. F3. Else probably O4.

11. P6. To many L3 would appear shrewder, but it is better to give up N3.

27. D2. To this it was usual to retort with

B	W
B2	C2
B3	but that lacks elegance.

32. D9. Far better than the hitherto customary E7 and exhibits depth of insight.

46. N10. If a player flees by means of a long sequence as White has done on line 12, his opponent must always follow. White does not play to make eyes by means of moves 41 to 51. If he should undertake to do this by means of L17, for example, then Black would threaten both incomplete positions by means of N14.

15. *Plate 110.*

16. R2. M4 is also good.

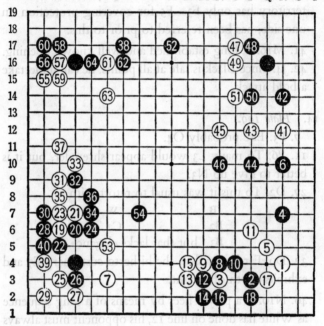

Plate 109

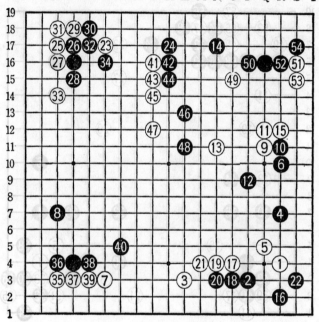

Plate 110

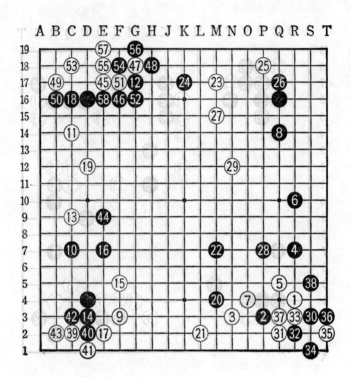

Plate 111

23. F17. The usual retort to this, C13, is not as good as 24 K17 which isolates F17.

16.   *Plate 111.*

21. L2. Black would do better not to retort to this.

28. P7. Very good. White can no longer play R12.

29. N12. Preferable to either P13 or P12.

38. S5. No advantage derives from the fact that Black lives in the corner, seeing that it only weakens him in the other positions.

17.   *Plate 112.*

7. R7. Previously it was usual in this case to play White L3, Black Q6.

27. C14. With this White sacrifices P3, 4, and if White retorts to Black 26 L3, it would entail

B	W
L3	M4
L4	M5
L5	M6
L6	M7
G4	and Black has a considerable ad-

vantage.

44. K2. See the note to 23 E2 in example 13 above.

18.   *Plate 113.*

9. R8. If 3 L3 were located at M3 or N3, then 9 Q7 should be played.

29. E14. That, in this case, Black's F15 follows upon 29 D14 has already been exhibited.

37. B12. Instead of this a beginner would play

A B C D E F G H J K L M N O P Q R S T

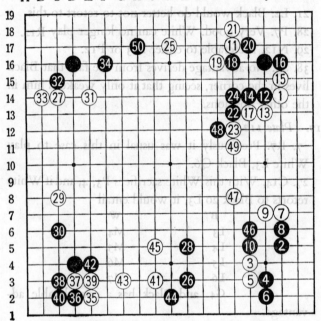

Plate 112

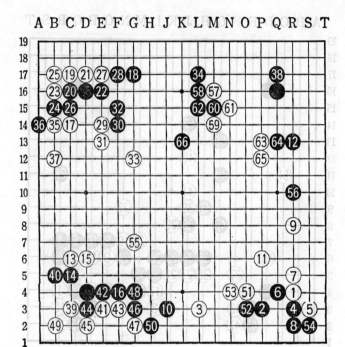

Plate 113

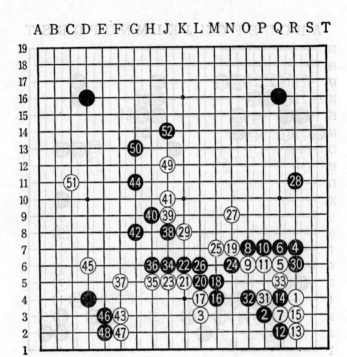

Plate 114

B	W
—	A13
A15	B12
E18	D18
F18	B19

and White is quite safe but Black has enlarged his territory.

50. H2. White is in fact alive in Black territory, but has positively no advantage from this.

19. *Plate 114.*

1. R4. All other openings are faulty.

8. O7. If Black plays 8 P4, then follows White 9 R6, Black 10 P6, White 11 P7 and there is promise of a hot skirmish. Black intentionally avoids this, though, because he finds himself already with the advantage and so under no circumstances can win anything further. It is always best for one to hold to the defensive as long as he has an advantageous position. This is a basic rule. The weaker player who always takes the Black stones and begins the game is, accordingly, at the opening in a position of advantage and should leave the attack to White. Later on, when White's superior game has obtained the greater prospect of victory, Black must do just the opposite and attack and, in fact, with all the more boldness the greater the disadvantage facing him. In chess this situation is reversed; in general, the stronger player or protagonist attacks and the weaker one remains on the defensive. I consider this one

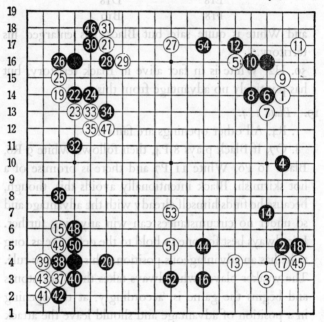

Plate 115

obtained the greater prospect of victory, Black must
do just the opposite and attack and, in fact, with all

of the greatest advantages that *Go* has over chess.
41. J10. Upon 41 H8 would come

B	W
G8	J7*
H7	J8
E6	—

51. C11. If White plays 51 J14, then Black occupies C10.

20. *Plate 115.*

27. K17. Upon 27 D15 would follow

B	W
E16	E15
F16	F15
G16	—

40. D3. 40 B5 would be incorrect, since line F is already occupied.

III. Black has a handicap of 2 stones.

21. *Plate 116.*

5. C11. 6 D16, 7 C8, is equally good as an opening.
20. E3. F5 is customary in this case, but Black wishes to reduce White's territory on the right.
48. R2. A very important move since Black knocks White out of eyes.

22. *Plate 117.*

9. C8. F17 is just as good, then follows Black G17, White F18.

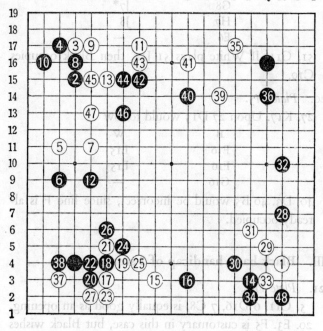

Plate 116

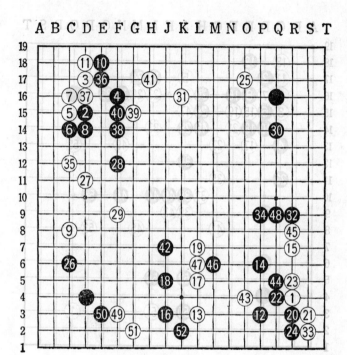

Plate 117

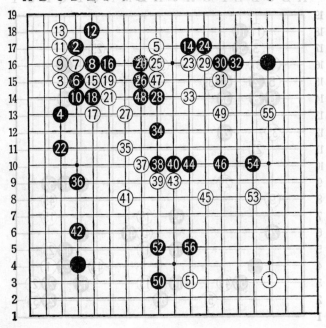

Plate 118

22. Q4. This and 24 R2 are needed because of White on line L.

28. F12. Very good, otherwise White plays E16 and tears up the Black position.

33. S2. Indeed now necessary to protect the White position around R6.

51. G2. Excellent. Thereby Black is forced to K2 and White can now play 53 F5 and as a result can flee, while without G2 White could have played only F4, whereupon Black would have cut him off with F6.

23. *Plate 118.*

14. L17. Black could now block White's next play E15 with 14 G15. But here the intention is to see how the game develops if White cuts.

19. F15. *Shi-cho** impossible since White occupies Q3.

20. H16. Makes the Black position secure.

50. J3. White cannot go over there without endangering his upper position.

56. L5. Black need not defend further his position E17 —P10, since it has two eyes certainly.

24. *Plate 119.*

19. B19. Appears more advantageous for White than it actually is, since L17 and C6 are yet to be protected.

*[*Shi-cho* refers to ladder tactics whereby an opponent's stones are checked alternately right and left and forced into a diagonal flight leading to the edge of the board and final capture. If the ladder leads to a previously placed opponent's stone, this tactic will not work and in fact will turn against the attacker. *Eds.*]

22. Q4. This and 24. R2 are needed because of White on line L.

28. F13. Very good, enlarging White play in B19 and tears up the Black position.

31. Indeed, how does Black to maintain his fighting spirit?

32. C8. The disadvantage of this strategy is that White will be allowed an even firmer grasp on the whole left side. While the influence of Z and Y is really good, Black may find it more valuable for the future to

38. B4. Black could, it may be, better be satisfied with a single, but he decides it wiser as to secure the entire lower left W are centre.

50. G9. Black ought with this step White to make up C4. Naturally. Then prospects seem to be equal.

27. R6.

31. R12. An error this two overrated

24. Plate 119.

19. B10. Appears more advantageous for White than it actually is, since L14 still are yet to be protected.

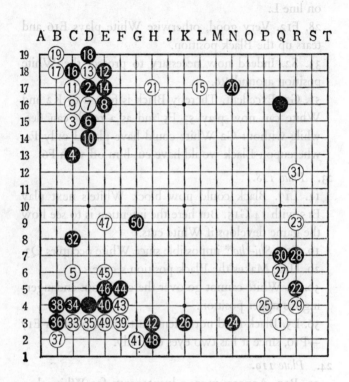

Plate 119

*Shi-dio refers to ladder tactics whereby an opponent's stones are checked alternately right and left and forced into a diagonal flight leading to the edge of the board and final capture. If the ladder leads to a previously placed opponent's stone, this tactic will not work and in fact will turn against the attacker. Eds.]

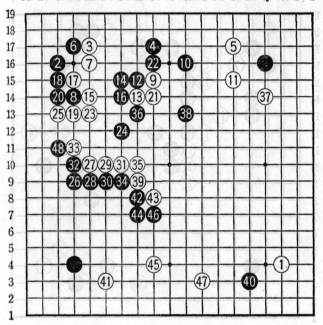

Plate 120

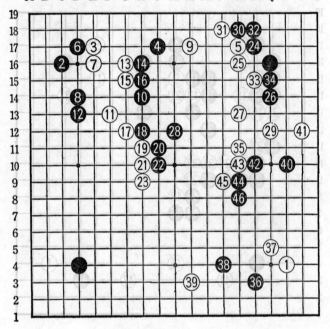

Plate 121

29. R4. P8 would be good, too, if 31 R12 were already in place.

50. G9. Black must play a keen game, because White has the advantage, otherwise D10 were also good.

25.   *Plate 120.*

11. O15. Usually one then plays Black Q14, but White would retort to that with L14.

24. G12. Attacks from both sides.

36. H13. In fact a strong attack, but Q14 would be still better.

42. H8. If the Black position at J16 were not so strong, D6 would have to be played.

48. C11. Were better not replied to.

26.   *Plate 121.*

12. D13. Customarily one plays D12 here, whence White E14, Black D15, White G12 follow.

20. J11. If the closed chain H14—16 were not there, then 20 J12 would be next.

26. Q14. White J12 is now impossible. One can see that

B	W
—	J12
H13	K12
F14	G14
G13	—

37. Q5. Customarily M3, then Black P6.

38. N4. Now White P7 would give to Black too much advantage with 40 J3.

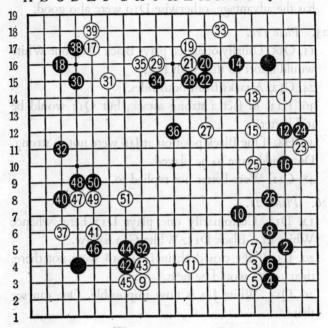

Plate 122

27. *Plate 122.*

5. P3. Following this, Black Q2, White L3 is also good.

9. H3. White cannot play 9 L3, since then Black R10 would follow.

12. R12. If O7 were not there, Black would go only to R10.

23. S11. Hinders Black from going to Q13 and is a neat play. One can see that

B	W
—	S11
Q13	Q14
P13	O13
O14	Q12
R13	R11

and the four Black stones are dead.

36. K12. Purely strategic in intention. The crucial effectiveness of this play can be appreciated in review after 52 H5.

28. *Plate 123.*

13. O4. White will then place R8. Black can respond to this by means of Q7, but this time the play develops in a more advantageous way.

18. S3. White R8 has now become purposeless.

28. N3. 28 F4 is usually played here, but N3 is better.

33. L5. Implies G4 instead of F4.

38. B15. Obstructs White C13.

40. D3. Black does well to dodge the skirmish that

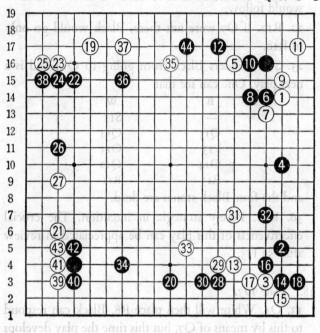

Plate 123

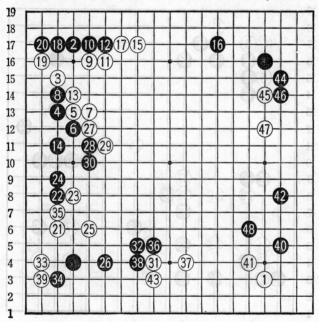

Plate 124

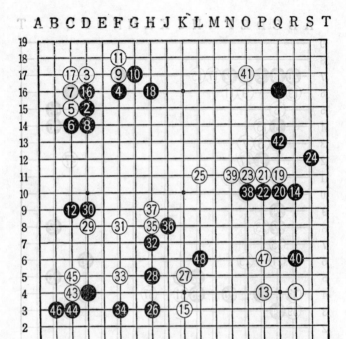

Plate 125

would ensue through 40 C4, and besides he retains Upperhand.

29. *Plate 124.*

   9. E16. Formerly D15 was usual.

   17. G17. For White to play B17 now would be absurd, for Black then goes to the right.

   31. J4. If F8 were also occupied by White, 31 would go toward H3.

   39. B3. White herewith abandons J4.

   48. P6. Will give rise to Black N4.

30. *Plate 125.*

   12. C9. Black intends to obtain much territory and so leaves the corner to White.

   18. H16. Exhibits the same design.

   25. L11. White avoids M11 and skips two spaces, since he is quite feeble.

   39. N11. Further struggle with White yields Black very little more; hence Black plays R6.

31. *Plate 126.*

   2. C16—4. D15. Quite old and the safest.

   14. R2. With that the Black position is secured.

   17. G3. Can be connected with L3 by means of J2. Black permits it in order to make a position with 18 F4.

   29. F7. Thereby White gives up C6.

   46. H15. Makes a very effective attack on White's position on line 14.

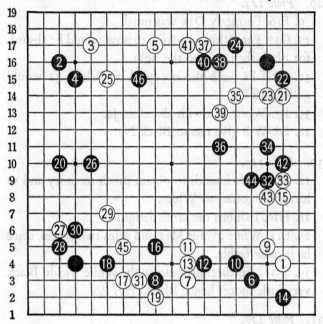

Plate 126

[232]

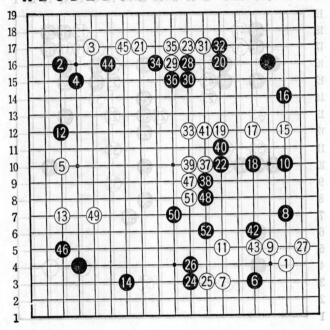

Plate 127

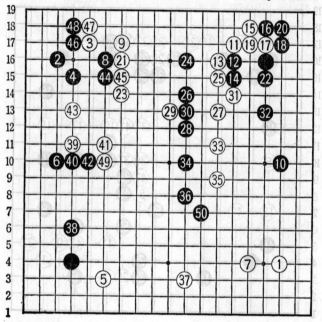

Plate 128

32. *Plate 127.*

11. N5. If no handicap had been allowed, White would play O4.

24. L3. If O4 had been played instead of N5, now White would play 25 C4.

27. S5. Otherwise would follow

B	W
S3	R3
R2	Q2
S1	T2
T3	Q3
S5	—

34. J16. Excellent, and one should note that this position often occurs.

52. M6. Exceptionally good. It accomplishes the essentially necessary connection of the two Black positions. We see that

B	W
M6	L7
L6	M7
N6	N7
O6	—

Black gives up two stones, but attains his purpose.

33. *Plate 128.*

22. Q15. Makes Black secure and allows him to anticipate L17.

36. L8. Black must reply here.

50. M7. White would still not be killed by N7.

34. *Plate 129.*

17. C10. Obstructs Black B5.

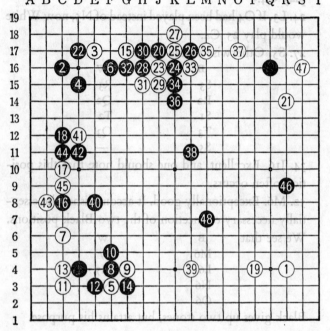

Plate 129

19. P4. Very important.

23. J16. Better than G16 because thereupon Black J15 would follow.

38. L11. Better than H13, as it gives connection with Q16.

39. L4. L3 is usual. But White goes a point higher to attack Black on lines K and L.

48. M7. Sharp indeed.

IV. Black has no handicap.

35. *Plate 130.*

12. O3. Then can follow

B	W
N3	P4
O2	P3
N4	Q6
R7	K3

But this is bad for Black.

15. N4. M3 would be just as good.

20. C11. White gives up E3—G3. If he played G4, then Black would seize C11 and Black would be too strong.

27. J5. Now the two White stones are isolated.

29. L15. Black can go no deeper.

36. *Plate 131.*

6. C11. Will spoil the aim of D5.

11. L17. In this case a distance of three spaces away is best. In earlier examples, M17 was played.

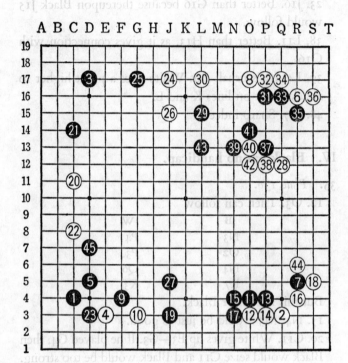

Plate 130

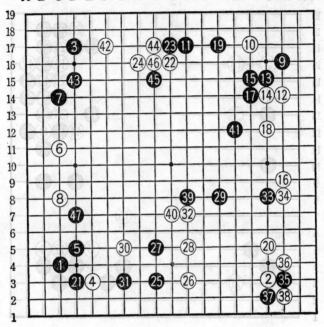

Plate 131

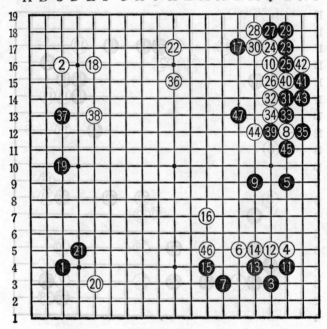

Plate 132

21. D3. Right on the spot. White C2 would have been very unpleasant for Black.

28. L5. It is now very difficult to penetrate farther into White territory.

29. N8. A play that only a few would dare to make since it lies entirely outside of routine techniques.

35. R3. A sacrifice.

37. Q2. As a consequence should follow

B	W
—	R2
P3	S3*
O5	which would give White the ad-

vantage.

37. *Plate 132.*

46. M5. Needed, because Black has become strong above.

47. O13. Now follows either 48 P13, 49 O15 or else 48 O15, 49 P13.

38. *Plate 133.*

14. Q6. If now follows Black M3, White would retort R11.

16. P17. White cannot play N3.

21. C14. Black avoids the engagement that would follow from 21 C7, 22 C13.

24. R13. With that White gives up C9. This is not usual, but justified by the condition that White is strong on line 5.

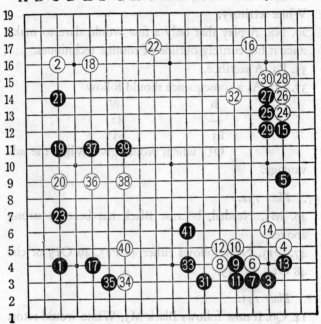

Plate 133

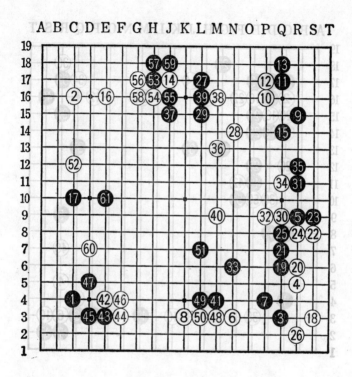

Plate 134

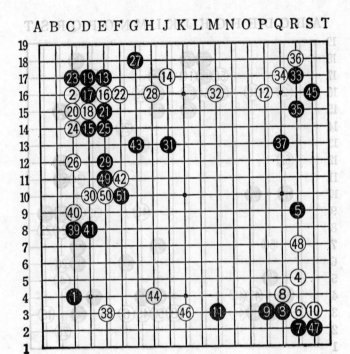

Plate 135

34. G3. Venturesome.

40. G5. G4 would be false.

41. L6. A very effective attack towards both sides.

39. *Plate 134.*

14. J17. L17 is conventional, but J17 takes into account that White already has occupied C16.

27. L17. Instead of this if Black had gone to O10, then White could not have cut him off at Q9, but he will have M16 and a considerable position in return.

43. E3. Black does not accept the sacrifice of N3.

40. *Plate 135.*

31. J13. This is an old play and a good one.

34. Q17. The usual retort is 35 R16 whence 36 R14 follows. 35 R15 is required by M16, and with it R17 is sacrificed immediately.

51. F10. The tough problem for White is now whether or not he should retain or sacrifice F11.

41. *Plate 136.*

27. N5. Without this play Black would lose.

29. C8. Instead of this D5 and then White C9 would have favored White too much.

39. G3. Can be occupied by Black, since he can above at right either make eyes with S14 or escape with N13.

51. C14. If now White seeks to save C12 by means of E12, then Black obtains G17. Hence, it is better to play 52 F17.

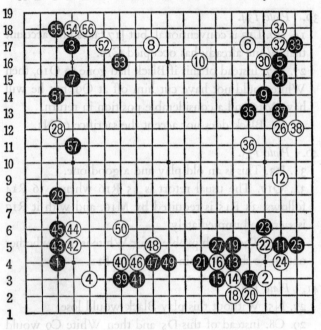

Plate 136

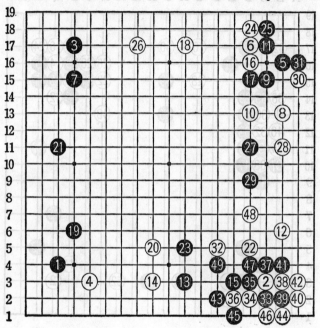

Plate 137

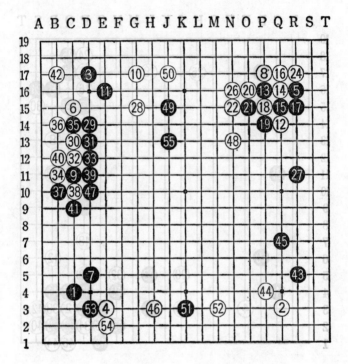

Plate 138

Ko 23 P16, 25 P15 Connects.

42. *Plate 137.*

12. R6. With this White abandons P17. Should Black play 13 K17, he would then retort with K3.

19. D6. Black will follow with G3.

24. P18. Very good, because of Upperhand.

31. S16. The variant 32 R9, 33 E11 would entail a very balanced meandering game; and, hence, White plays N5.

43. *Plate 138.*

15. Q15. Since Black does not hold possession of L17, he sacrifices P16 and will take Q14.

42. B17. White lives. Black could also let White escape; it makes no difference.

55. J13. If Black were not quite strong in the lower left, he would have to play K5.

44. *Plate 139.*

10. C11. White is unable to play 10 G3, because Black would then occupy C11.

18. C8. Gives up C15.

25. R9. 25 Q18 would bring about 26 R8.

33. S7. Connects R5 and R9.

34. E4. With that E3 is rescued.

44. N13. Obstructs Black from cutting at N15 and Q13.

45. *Plate 140.*

7. D5. Were Black to play C15 instead of this, White would obtain the advantage. We see that

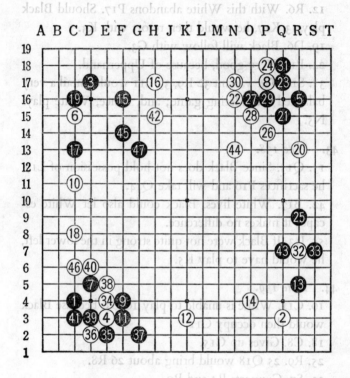

Plate 139

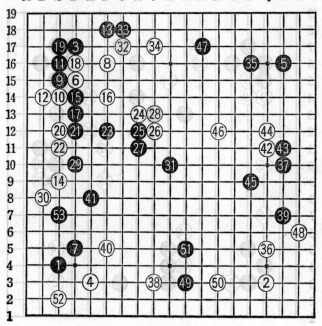

Plate 140

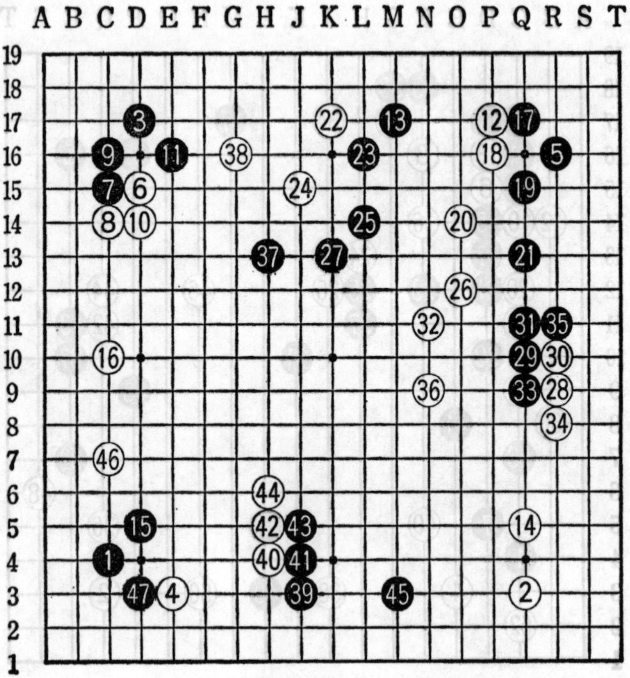

Plate 141

B	W
C15	C14
C16	D14
E16	C7
D5	E7

12. B14. Forces Black to retort at left above. Upon 12 D14 Black would follow with C9.

41. E8. Prevents White from cutting at J11 and helps Black C4—D5 to escape.

47. M17. If White now plays M4, then Black would answer with S5.

46. *Plate 141.*

45. M3. Better than N3. After 45 N3, White H3 is Upperhand.

47. *Plate 142.*

19. H18. Far better than G17.

33. G12. 33 H14 would be bad.

46. R17. A sacrifice.

48. *Plate 143.*

23. C9. Hitherto one always played J17 here.

33. R13. Should Black play R12, White can retort R14. 33 R13, however, permits Black to attack later with R8.

This opening has a very simple formation.

49. *Plate 144.*

14. R4. Sacrifices E3.

30. L18 and 31. N17. Both serve as sacrifices.

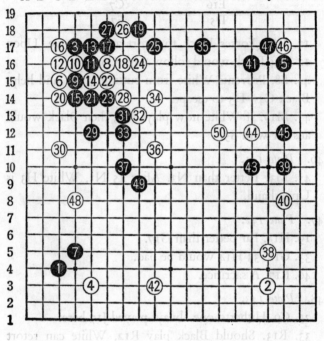

Plate 142

33. R13. Should Black play R13, White can retort R12. 33 R13, however, permits black to attack later with R8.

This opening has a very simple formation.

49. Plate 144.

14. R11. Sacrifices I3.

30. L15 and 31. N17. Both serve as sacrifices.

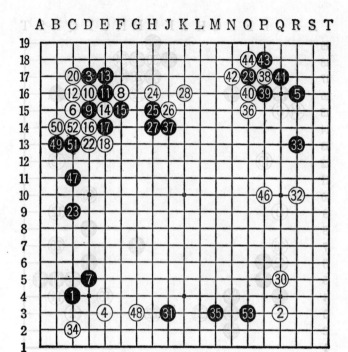

Plate 143

Ko 19 D15, 21 E15 Connects; 45 P17 Connects.

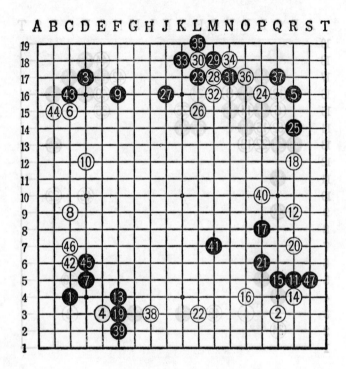

Plate 144

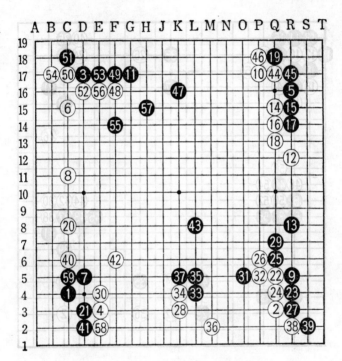

Plate 145

[A board of 21 ×21 lines.]

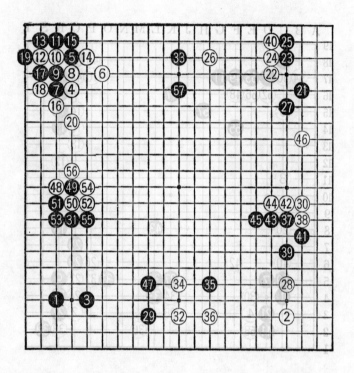

Plate 146

[A board of 21 × 21 lines.]

50. *Plate 145.*

44. Q17. Quite as good as J17 after which Black plays P18.

59. C5. Otherwise White plays B5, Black B4, White B2 and Black is dead.

V. A 21-line board.

I have mentioned before that the size of the board was fixed at 19 lines only after a variety of tests with other sizes. In fact I have been informed that the board had only 18 lines when *Go* arrived in Japan, but soon afterward was increased to 19. This was obviously an improvement, since with an odd number of lines the board breaks up into symmetrical areas. To see if the game would be improved if the board were enlarged still further, I had one prepared with 21 lines and turned it over to the Master for testing. See Plate 146 [in which a board of 21×21 lines is depicted with a suggested development of 57 moves]. It was evident that the game took on a freer and more deeply involved character, but that at the same time the difficulty of keeping command of the game grew at an extraordinary rate. To this one must add that the game lasted longer; some 70 more stones were played. The 21-line board appeared to have a future, but it could only be appropriately used by expert players. With the 19-line board, as it is, too many unexpected situations turn up for beginners. Were the board increased to 23 lines or more, not even the best players could any longer maintain a comprehensive view of the countless possible combinations. Boards of the 23-line form can, then, be left until such time as the human understanding has become better disciplined for *Go* combinations than is the case at present.

V. A 21-line board.

EXTRINSIC NOTES

EXTRINSIC NOTES

1. *Shogi* is well organized in Japan today, and has an accumulated documentation, including a book in English entitled *Japanese Chess,* by E. Ohara, Charles E. Tuttle Co., Tokyo and Rutland, Vermont, 1958. Adherents of the game deny that it is impossible to plan an overall strategy effectively.

2. *Mill:* A space game, played either on an outside court or on an arranged board. See *morris* (not the dance), *Webster's Unabridged Dictionary.*

3. Not today, of course. This refers to Korschelt's time in Japan, shortly after the Meiji Restoration.

4. Korschelt's time references should be reckoned from about the first decade of the last quarter of the 19th century.

5. There now exists a Japan *Go* Association, organized in 1924, with headquarters in Tokyo, and this is the capital authority on the game. *Go* clubs are now being promoted and fostered throughout the world with the active assistance of the Japan *Go* Association, principally through the sponsorship of tours by professional *Go*

players from Japan. A European *Go* Tournament has been held annually for some six years. The First International *Go* Tournament was held in Tokyo in October, 1963 (the Japan team won). For those desiring to make further inquiries, the address of the Association is: Nihon Ki-In (Japan *Go* Association), 5th floor, Kokusai-Kanko Building, No. 1, 1-chome, Marunouchi, Chiyoda-ku, Tokyo. There is an American organization which maintains close liaison with the Japan Association and which may be reached at: The American *Go* Association, 145 West 57 Street, New York, New York.

6. Murase Shuho (1838-1886 A.D.), the 18th Hon-In-Bo, a cognomen of traditional order and of distinguished proficiency. See notes 12 and 14 below.

7. Japanese words and names are spelled according to the Hepburn System, without marking long vowels; Chinese, according to the Wade-Giles System. Dates for Japanese periods and events conform with the *Historical and Geographical Dictionary of Japan,* Edmond Papinot, Overbeck Co., Ann Arbor, Michigan, 1948. Chinese periods and events are dated according to the orthodox traditions. Korschelt used slightly different dates and names.

8. For an interesting account of major Japanese names and events mentioned by Korschelt, see, for instance, George Sansom's *A History of Japan to 1334* and *A History of Japan 1334-1615,* Stanford University Press. See also

Stuart Culin's *Games of the Orient*, Charles E. Tuttle Company, 1958. It has not been possible to identify some of the persons named by Korschelt; for example, "Osan" is probably a term of formal respect and not a proper name while other names do not seem to be part of the main stream of Japanese or Chinese military and political history as usually written. Some of the renderings are obviously Japanese pronunciations of Chinese names.

9. It is customary for the authorities of the Nihon Ki-In to contract with newspapers for professional *Go* tournaments. A newspaper publishing company will put up game fees and other expense monies in return for the exclusive right to publish the tournament games, which usually appear in serial form. Annual tournaments include the Hon-In-Bo, Meijin, Ju-Dan, and Oza contests. Participants in Asahi Shimbun's unique Professional Best Ten Tournament are selected by popular vote. Amateur *Go* tournaments find similar backing, as for example the Amateur Hon-In-Bo Tournament sponsored by the Mainichi Shimbun.

10. Sansha was originally a Buddhist monk, named Nikkai. His vocational name, Hon-In-Bo, was inherited in turn by disciples, judged as best, one generation after another, in the Hon-In-Bo school of play. The title of champion was bestowed upon him by Nobunaga. Those who held the title of champion thereafter and until 1940 are: Nakamura Doseki, 1st Nakamura; Yasui Sanchi,

2nd Yasui; Hon-In-Bo Dosaku, 4th Hon-In-Bo; Inouye Inseki, 4th Inouye; Hon-In-Bo Dochi, 5th Hon-In-Bo; Hon-In-Bo Sakugen, 9th Hon-In-Bo; Hon-In-Bo Jowa, 12th Hon-In-Bo; Hon-In-Bo Shuei, 17th Hon-In-Bo; and Hon-In-Bo Shusai, 21st Hon-In-Bo.

11. A *tsubo*=6 sq. *shaku*. A *shaku*=a Japanese foot= 11 $^{15}/_{16}$ U.S. inches. A *koku*=4.96 bushels. This is an exchange system based on land and its rice-yield, thus indicative of an economic order primarily formulated in agrarian measures. For an attempt to relate this to money values see Appendix II to Saikaku's *The Life of An Amorous Woman*, edited and translated by Ivan Morris, 1963, a New Directions Book.

12. As of 1939, the Japan *Go* Association, under the leadership of Hon-In-Bo Shusai, was predominant. A remnant of the Inouye School persisted at Osaka, and other dispersed groups were active. As for the name Hon-In-Bo, however, though the school lasted in a line of continuous inheritance from master of the school to favored disciple until Hon-In-Bo Shusai, 21st Hon-In-Bo, he freed it from its "familial" succession in 1937. Since then the title has been awarded by means of a tournament sponsored by the Press, thus recapturing something of its original status as a game played before the Shogun—except now the Public has implicitly replaced the August Presence.

13. The *Sho* in *Sho-dan* means not so much "one" as

"beginning." The other prefixes of *dan* are numerical terms, however. As of December 1963 there were fifteen players of the Ninth Rank, all in Japan, fourteen of Japanese ancestry and one of Chinese ancestry.

14. Murase Shuho (1838-1886 A.D.), 18th Hon-In-Bo, and Korschelt's teacher. Thus it is not difficult to infer that the Hon-In-Bo School, which held the majority of championship titles, exercised a major influence on Korschelt.

15. Möllendorff's *Chinese Bibliography:* A list of works and essays, relating to China, by P. G. and O. F. Möllendorff; Shanghai, Kelly and Walsh; London, Trübner & Co., 1876, 378 pp.; lists German, French and English titles. Korschelt was perhaps not in a position to investigate this matter thoroughly. There is, for instance, a book on *Go* in Chinese, entitled: *Yuan Yuan Ch'i Ching* (元元棋経), presumed to have been written by Yen Tien Chang, of the Yüan Dynasty (1606-1628 A.D.). This was about the time Descartes was writing his *Meditations* in the West.

16. *Salisburia adiantifolia:* in Japanese, *Icho,* or *Gingko.* But for further details on this topic, see: *The Game of* GO, Arthur Smith, Charles E. Tuttle Co., Tokyo and Rutland, Vermont; Ch. II, pp. 18-19.

17. Korschelt has probably not been apt about the proper *Ko*-ideogram here: 劫, which by some is taken to be the one for "endless time," although Rose-Innes refers it back to 刧 meaning "to threaten," "to menace," "to plunder." But so far as the contemporary game is concerned these analogues do not matter, since the operation named *Ko* is exhibited by Korschelt clearly. Strictly speaking, it is a virtue of Korschelt's analytic exposition that names are imposed as nominal tags on typical operations and do not stand for the sort of synthetic intuitions evoked by ideograms. In this sense the word *Ko* is not essentially Japanese but the name of a typical operation in the glossary of *Go*.

18. The Editors have added Rules 6, 7, and 8 to fill out the minimum exposition given by Korschelt. Rule 6 is the situation known as *Seki* illustrated on Plate 28 in connection with Game X. Rule 7 is purely arbitrary and has been the subject of much debate. Rule 8 is necessary in order that players of unequal strength may oppose each other. Rule 3 is the situation known as *Ko*. There are special rules covering more complicated *Ko* situations (e.g. triple and quadruple *Ko* patterns), but these are not likely to be necessary in the early stages of one's acquaintance with the game. The *Go* Rules established by the Japan *Go* Association run to 70 sections grouped under 10 headings.

19. Today's usage is just the opposite: Japanese numerals or English alphabet from top to bottom, and Arabic numerals from left to right. See Rule III (9) (ii) of the *Go* Rules established by the Japan *Go* Association. However, others still use Korschelt's system; for example, Takagawa in his book *The Vital Points of* GO, Japan *Go* Association *(Nihon Ki-In)*, Tokyo, 1958.